# The Comparison Detox

Unfollow the Noise.

Reclaim Your Voice

**Belle Titmus**

# Dedication

For anyone who's ever looked around and felt like they were falling behind—

this is your reminder that your life isn't supposed to look like theirs.

It's supposed to *feel* like yours.

# Acknowledgment

To the person I once was—

The one who measured every milestone, every mirror, and every moment against someone else's "better" or "enough."

Thank you for surviving the ache of comparison, for all the times you scrolled and sighed and shrank, yet still got up and tried again. Thank you for being honest about your longing, your envy, your fear of missing out, and your quiet hope that maybe, one day, you could feel good in your own skin.

Thank you for asking, "What if my life could be enough?"— even when the world told you to keep chasing, keep hustling, keep comparing.

I see your exhaustion. I honor your resilience. I forgive your self-doubt.Because of you, I learned that compassion is stronger than judgment, and that the courage to stay in your own lane is the most radical act of all. You taught me that real belonging starts with coming home to myself— messy, unfinished, and deeply human.

To the version of me who once believed everyone else was ahead: thank you for holding on. Thank you for being the starting place, the soft ground on which I could finally plant my own roots.

This book—and this life—are dedicated to your journey.

You were never behind.

You were always becoming.


With love and gratitude,
Belle

# Table of Contents

# ✦ Introduction ✦

## When the Mirror Becomes a Measuring Tape

*Why We Compare, How It Wounds Us, and What It Means to Finally Unfollow the Noise*

You know that subtle ache in your chest after scrolling past someone else's highlight reel—the one that says, "I should be further along by now"? It's not a scream, not even a shout. It's softer, sneakier, the kind of voice that slips in through the cracks when you're tired, bored, or just waiting for your coffee to cool. That's comparison.

Comparison doesn't need a megaphone. It's a master of disguise—a chameleon in your psyche. One minute, it's masquerading as motivation ("Maybe if I worked harder, I'd have what she has"), the next, it's whispering doubts so quietly you almost mistake them for your own inner wisdom. It loves to show up at the most inconvenient times: when you're standing in your kitchen eating cold pizza over the sink, when you're trying to juggle work emails and your kid's science project, when you just want to enjoy your own damn life without feeling like you're auditioning for an invisible panel of judges.

That moment when someone else's sun-dappled vacation photo, business launch announcement, toned arms, storybook proposal, or minimalist kitchen seeps into your bones and settles there—not as inspiration, but as a kind of quiet failure? That's not just jealousy, darling. That's grief in disguise. That's the aching internal alarm that asks, "Why not me?" Or, on the rougher days, "What's wrong with me?"

Let's be clear: comparison isn't a flaw in your character. It's not proof that you're petty, ungrateful, or shallow. It's a function of your humanity, baked right into your DNA from the days when we all lived in small bands and needed to know our place in the pecking order so we wouldn't get left out in the cold with the sabre-toothed tigers.

But while comparison might be universal, it's also a thief. It's the pickpocket of your joy, your energy, your voice, your time, and your connection to the actual, unfiltered life you're living. It steals quietly but persistently, siphoning away self-acceptance and leaving you with a constant sense of not enoughness.

Here's the good news: this book is about breaking that spell. About slipping out of comparison's grasp—not by pretending you don't care (you do, and that's okay), not by deleting every app and moving to the forest (though listen, if that's your vibe, I support you), and definitely not by shaming yourself for having these thoughts in the first place. This is about reclaiming your own damn lane, painting your own finish line, and finally feeling at home in your life again—even if it looks nothing like the ones you see online.

## Why We're All Tired (and Don't Even Know It)

Modern life is a relentless onslaught of information, images, and updates. We're living in an era that offers more access to other people's lives than any generation before us. You don't just see your friends anymore. You see everyone—their bodies, their homes, their careers, their relationships, their Sunday morning pancakes, their skincare routines, and yes, even their dog's daily affirmations.

You are bombarded, from the minute you wake up to the moment your head hits the pillow, with perfectly filtered lives, curated captions, and carefully timed humblebrags. Even when you know—intellectually—that it's not the whole story, that there's a mess just outside the frame, your nervous system doesn't. Your body sees only the highlight reel, and it translates it into a story about your own lack.

"She's thriving."
"I'm behind."
"She's got it together."
"I'm a mess."
"They're winning."
"I'm invisible."

And even when you do root yourself, ground yourself, light your candles, and recite your mantras, comparison creeps back in. Because we've been trained, over and over, to use other people's lives as a mirror. But somewhere along the way, that mirror turned into a measuring tape. And, let's be honest, it's strangling us.

# What Comparison Does to the Mind and Body

Let's pull back the curtain for a minute. Comparison isn't just a mental game—it's a full-body experience. When you compare, your brain activates its threat response. The primitive part of your mind interprets someone else's success, beauty, stability, or visibility as evidence of your own lack, as danger, as a sign that you might be left behind. In the ancient world, your social standing could mean survival or exile. So your brain still scans for where you stand, even if the stakes are now just digital likes and comments.

The problem? You're ranking yourself in a game you never agreed to play, measuring your becoming against someone else's curated moment, comparing your day-to-day mess to someone else's polished press release. And then, unsurprisingly, you end up feeling like a failure.

But here's the real kicker: comparison isn't just unkind; it's untrue. It's a faulty lens, a broken ruler. Unlearning it isn't about pretending you're above it—it's about detoxing from a system that profits off your self-doubt, that keeps you endlessly scrolling, buying, and hustling for worth you already have.

## What This Book Is (and What It Isn't)

This is not a book about pretending you're a lone wolf who doesn't give a damn about what people think. You care. Of course you do—because you're human, not a robot. Caring isn't the problem. Using someone else's path as the measure of your worth? That's the problem.

This book is here to help you:

- Uncover the root of your comparison triggers (because yes, they have roots)
- Recognize the emotional hangover that follows the scroll (and how to recover)
- Understand how envy, when listened to, can actually point you toward what you really want (spoiler: you're not a monster for feeling it)
- Separate your self-worth from timelines, bodies, followers, and curated "success"
- Reclaim your voice, your vision, and your values (even if you feel like you lost them somewhere between the hashtags)

- Learn how to actually like your life again—even if it looks nothing like hers, his, or theirs

Within these pages, you'll find reflection prompts, rituals, mini-missions, and perspective shifts woven into every chapter. Not to fix you (because, let me be clear, you were never broken), but to help you return to yourself. Because the only thing that's really been wrong all this time is the story that says your life should look like someone else's.

## A Soft Invitation Before We Begin

You're allowed to want what you want.
You're allowed to feel the sting of envy.
You're allowed to feel behind, left out, or not quite "there."
You're allowed to crave more, to wish for different, to imagine better.

But you're also allowed—starting right now—to unsubscribe from the story that says your life isn't valid unless it looks like hers. You're allowed to define enoughness on your own terms, to love your life—even if it's quiet, weird, slow, messy, or blooming on a timeline no one else understands.

This is your lane. This is your life. And it's time to come home to it—fully, loudly, beautifully, with all your quirks, detours, and unfinished drafts. Because the world doesn't need another copy of someone else. It needs a fully embodied, deeply alive, unapologetically you.

So let's detox from the comparison. Let's unfollow the noise. Let's reclaim the joy of being you.

Ready? Let's begin.

# ✦Chapter 1✦

## The Comparison Hangover

*What Happens When You Measure Your Life by Someone Else's Highlight Reel*

There's a kind of exhaustion that doesn't come from hustling too hard, logging too many hours, or even from wrangling sticky toddlers or sitting in endless meetings that could have been emails. No, this exhaustion is subtler, sneakier. It doesn't show up as bags under your eyes or sore muscles. It's the quiet, persistent drain that comes from measuring your life against someone else's—usually without even realizing you're doing it.

You know the drill. You open your phone "just for a minute," and suddenly your thumb is on autopilot, scrolling through a parade of engagement rings, six-figure launches, glowing skin, and sun-flared vacation shots with hashtags like #livingmybestlife. Your coffee goes cold, your heart goes numb, and your mind starts its greatest hits playlist: "She's so far ahead," "Why can't I get it together?" "Everyone else is thriving, and I'm… here."

You scroll.
You sigh.
You shrink.

You tell yourself it's harmless, a little digital window shopping for inspiration. You're "just catching up," right? But your heart tells a different story. Even when you know it's curated, even when you know people only post their best moments, you still feel the ache. You still feel behind. Less than. Off track. Invisible. And afterward? You don't feel motivated or connected, or inspired. You feel like someone drained your joy and replaced it with shame.

That's the comparison hangover.
It's not loud. It doesn't scream. It creeps in quietly after a binge on someone else's life, leaving you with a subtle, sticky emotional residue—a sense that your own ordinary, extraordinary, messy, beautiful life isn't enough.

## This Isn't Weakness. It's Programming.

Before you start diagnosing yourself with another character flaw, let's get one thing straight: comparison doesn't make you shallow. It makes you human. Really, really human.

Your brain is a pattern-recognition machine. It's constantly scanning your environment to figure out where you belong and how safe you are. Back in the day—like, way back, saber-toothed-tiger-back—this kept us alive. You needed to know who was faster, stronger, or better at foraging. Your place in the tribe could mean survival, comfort, or exile.

Now, instead of competing for berries or the best cave, your brain's ancient wiring is being hijacked by algorithms, filters, and the endless scroll. Your nervous system doesn't know the difference between an actual threat and a perceived one. So when you see someone who looks more successful, more radiant, or more "ahead," your brain interprets it as social danger. It triggers a low-level sense of failure, lack, and even the fear of being left behind.

And when this happens, not just once but dozens—maybe hundreds—of times a day, you don't just compare. You contract. You shrink. You start to build your life around someone else's outline, always wondering what's wrong with yours.

It's not your fault. It's just your brain, trying to keep you safe… in a world that's gone from campfires to comment sections.

## The Sneaky Signs of a Comparison Hangover

Here's the thing about a comparison hangover: it doesn't announce itself. There's no "alert" or handy notification. It's subtle, insidious, and often disguised as everyday feelings.

How do you know you've been hit? Here are the telltale symptoms:

- **You feel like your wins aren't real unless someone else acknowledges them.**
  That brilliant idea at work? Meh, it only counts if it's trending. The home-cooked meal you're proud of? Not impressive unless it's Pinterest-worthy. Your own joy starts to feel conditional, dependent on external validation.

- **You suddenly dislike your body, your home, your work, or your entire life.**
Five minutes ago, you were feeling okay about your jeans, your living room, your career. Then you saw someone else's "after" photo or boho-chic decor, and now everything you have seems "less than." (Spoiler: nothing actually changed but your perspective.)

- **You start mentally tallying where you 'should' be by now.**
Shouldn't you own a house? Shouldn't you have a ring? Shouldn't you have a bestselling side hustle and a wardrobe that matches your mood board? The "shoulds" multiply, crowding out gratitude and suffocating the joy of your own timeline.

- **You hesitate to share your own joy because it feels small in comparison.**
That thing you wanted to post about? Suddenly it feels silly, so you keep it to yourself. You dim your light rather than risk being seen as "less impressive."

- **You find yourself irritable, unmotivated, or drained for no clear reason.**
You can't quite put your finger on it, but you're

just "off." You feel restless, anxious, or inexplicably tired. Your creativity stalls. You lose your appetite for your own life.

It's not that you're broken. It's that your joy got interrupted—by someone else's projected perfection. And now? You're disconnected from the only life that's actually yours.

## A Story from the Scroll

Let's get real for a minute. Here's how it tends to play out:

It's Sunday morning. You're on your couch, coffee in hand, still in pajamas. You open your phone, promising yourself, "just five minutes." Two swipes in, you see your college roommate's engagement photos. Three more scrolls, and a former coworker is announcing a book deal. Next, an influencer's kitchen renovation looks like a page out of a magazine. Your heart rate picks up. Your coffee suddenly tastes bitter.

You look around your own living room. The laundry is piled up, the dog is shedding, your "romantic partner" is snoring on the couch, and you're not even sure what you're doing with your life. You started the morning feeling fine—maybe even grateful. But by the time you put your phone down, your mood has soured. You're not inspired to take action. You're inspired to crawl back into bed.

That's the comparison hangover in action. It's not about what you see—it's about what you make it mean.

## The Energy Drain of Measuring Everything

Every moment you spend comparing is a moment you're not present in your own story. It's emotional labor you never signed up for, and it's exhausting.

Let's break down the hidden costs:

- **Measuring your timeline against hers:** She's married, you're not. She's got a promotion, you're still figuring out your next move. Suddenly, your timeline is "off," even though there's no universal clock.
- **Analyzing her post like a detective:** You zoom in on her vacation photos, trying to spot

signs of Photoshop or cracks in the facade. You read between the lines, crafting stories about her happiness or how she "must have it all together."

- **Deciding you should change something that was perfectly fine five minutes ago:**
  You were happy with your kitchen until you saw her marble countertops. You were proud of your progress until you saw her "transformation." You start shopping for things you never wanted, hustling for goals you never chose.

- **Shaping your choices around someone else's version of 'enough':**
  You plan your life like it's a game of catch-up. You say yes to things that don't light you up. You say no to things that do, because they're not on someone else's highlight reel.

The result?

You're left in emotional debt.

Comparison robs you of clarity, creativity, motivation, self-trust, and the simple enjoyment of the actual life you're living. And, worst of all, you forget who you are when you're not busy being everyone else.

# The Science: Why It Hurts So Much

Let's nerd out for a second. When you compare, your brain releases stress hormones like cortisol. Your body registers the perceived threat, even if it's just a picture of someone else's salad. Over time, these micro-stresses add up, leaving you feeling tired, anxious, and disconnected.

Psychologists call this "social comparison theory." In a nutshell, we evaluate ourselves by looking at others—usually those we perceive as "above" us in some way. This might have helped us fit in with our tribe, but now it leaves us perpetually dissatisfied. The rise of social media has only intensified the effect, giving us endless opportunities to compare and despair.

## Spotting the Hangover: A Reflection Break

Time for some radical honesty. Grab your journal, a napkin, or just pause and check in with yourself. Answer these, no filter:

1. **Where do you feel comparison the most?**
   Is it scrolling through social media, catching up

with friends, in your career, your body, your relationships?

2. **What do you tell yourself in those moments?**

   Are the stories kind, or are they secretly savage? Are you using someone else's success as proof of your "failure"?

3. **How does your mood shift after scrolling or consuming someone else's "success"?**

   Do you feel inspired, or do you feel smaller? Is there a heaviness, a little cloud following you through the day?

4. **What parts of your life do you suddenly feel ashamed of—even though they brought you peace before?**

   What did you love about your life before comparison snuck in?

Now, the big one:

**Who are you when you're not trying to match someone else's timeline, appearance, or energy?**
Sit with that. You might find that you actually like that

version of you—unfiltered, unranked, unbothered—way more than the one always playing catch-up.

## The Cost of the Hangover: What You're Really Giving Up

Let's name what's at stake. Every time you measure your life against someone else's, you're not just losing time. You're leaking energy, confidence, and possibility.

- **You lose clarity.** Your own dreams get fuzzy. You forget what you wanted before everyone else's wants filled your field of vision.
- **You lose creativity.** Comparison is a creativity killer. Instead of making something new, you're stuck copying, tweaking, or resenting.
- **You lose motivation.** Why bother trying if you're already "behind"? The joy of the process gets replaced by the anxiety of the finish line.
- **You lose self-trust.** You second-guess your choices, your timing, your taste. You outsource your confidence to strangers with cute dogs and curated feeds.

- **You lose the pleasure of your own life.** You stop noticing the good stuff happening right now, at your kitchen table, in your messy, magical, very human life.

And the biggest loss?
**You lose yourself.**
And babe, that's too high a price for a little digital window shopping.

## Mini Detox Practice: A 24-Hour Comparison Cleanse

Let's not just talk about it—let's do something about it.

For one day, try this experiment. Think of it as a little reset button for your nervous system:

- **No checking who's doing what.** Log off. Mute the noise. If you must peek, set a timer.
- **No scrolling for "inspiration."** Inspiration is great, but if it leaves you feeling less, it's time to take a break.

- **No peeking at your competitors, exes, or that girl from high school with the curated kitchen.**
- **No self-ranking.** No tallying up wins and losses, no mental Olympics.

Instead:

- **Write down three things you're proud of— even if no one knows about them.**
  Maybe it's the way you handled a tough conversation, the garden you're growing, the fact that you showed up for yourself today.
- **Pay attention to your own life: your body, your home, your creativity, your breath.**
  Notice what feels good, what brings you peace, what makes you laugh. Savor it.
- **Celebrate yourself out loud—like you're your own hype woman, because... you are.**
  Try it in the mirror. Try it in the shower. Try it while making coffee. "Damn, I'm resilient." "Look at me go." "I'm showing up."

Notice how your energy shifts when you stop importing everyone else's lives into your nervous system. It won't be perfect. You'll probably catch yourself reaching for the phone, craving a quick hit of "How am I doing?" That's okay. You're not failing; you're just building a new muscle—presence over performance.

## The Secret to a Comparison-Free Life (Spoiler: It's Not Perfection)

Let's get one thing straight: you don't owe the world a better version of you. You don't need to match her highlight reel. You don't have to apologize for your slower, quieter, messier, truer timeline. Your lane was never meant to look like hers.

Some days, you'll slip up. You'll scroll, you'll sigh, you'll shrink. But you'll also remember that your life is not a competition. It's a masterpiece in progress—one that doesn't need a filter, a like, or anyone else's stamp of approval.

So here's your permission slip:
To rest. To root. To return to yourself.
To let your own story be enough.
To celebrate the small wins, the slow mornings, the ordinary joys.

To trust that the only person you're meant to become... is yourself.

Your presence is your revolution. Your life, lived fully, is your rebuttal to the tyranny of comparison.

This is your lane.
Stay in it.
Make it wild, make it yours, make it home.

# ✦Chapter 2✦

## Scroll. Sigh. Repeat.

*How Social Media Became a Mirror That Always Says "Not Enough"*

Let's start with a brutal truth:

You didn't wake up today saying, "You know what would really spice up my morning routine? A little dose of self-doubt and existential dread by breakfast." No one plans to compare. No one adds "feel like a failure" to the to-do list.

And yet, here we are.

You opened an app. That's it. That's all it took.

Five minutes of "just checking in"—maybe to see if your friend liked your meme, or to check if your favorite dog account posted—morphed into thirty minutes of slow-drip insecurity. You watched as someone you barely know posted their perfect kitchen, all marble and sunbeams, not a crumb in sight. You saw her spontaneous weekend getaway, complete with the kind of travel outfit that suggests she floats, not sweats. Her engagement shoot—somewhere magical, with perfectly wind-blown hair. Her post-baby abs, because apparently, some people bounce back like rubber bands. Her thriving business announcement. Her cottagecore morning matcha, all affirmations, and natural lighting, and a type of calm that feels like a personal attack.

And you? You're just trying to brush your teeth before noon, wearing a t-shirt that's seen better decades and socks that don't match. Your breakfast is... whatever you found in the fridge. Your affirmations are more like, "Don't forget deodorant."

You didn't ask to feel like a failure.
But somehow, you left your feed with your joy bruised and your worth dented, like a banana at the bottom of a backpack.

Welcome to the scroll spiral—aka, the world's most addictive, soul-numbing comparison machine.

This chapter isn't about shaming your screen time. Lord knows we don't need more guilt in our lives. This is about exposing the lie: the one that says everyone else is winning, and you're not even in the race.
Let's drag that lie out into the sunlight, shall we?

# The Illusion of Being "Connected"

Let's not demonize social media entirely. It's a tool, and like all tools, its impact depends on how we use it—or, more accurately, how it uses us.

Here's what social media promises:
Connection. Community. Inspiration. A portal to friends, family, and strangers who feel like friends. A place to cheer each other on, to share our stories, to learn, to laugh, to be seen.

And sometimes, that's true. Sometimes, you really do find a community, a friend, a moment of genuine connection. But mixed into the digital soup is something much more slippery: a system built to monetize your attention.

Not your joy.
Not your presence.
Not your peace.

Every swipe, like, and click is tracked and optimized—not to connect you, but to keep you hungry. Keep you reaching. Keep you scrolling, searching for a life that looks shinier than the one you're living. The more you scroll, the more you feed the machine. The machine, in turn, feeds you back a highlight reel of other people's wins, never their wounds.

So what happens?
You compare real life—messy, beautiful, unfiltered—to edited life.
Your blooper reel to someone else's highlight montage.
Your vulnerable moments to someone else's filtered feed.

And the result is rarely inspiration. It's depletion.

## The "Comparison Algorithm"

Let's get nerdy for a second. You know those algorithms—the mysterious digital elves that decide what you see when you open an app? Here's their job: keep you engaged. They notice when you pause, what you like, what makes you linger. If you spend five seconds longer on that influencer's #vanlife post, poof! Suddenly your feed is all perfectly staged road trips. You click on a post about fitness, and now every scroll is a parade of abs and green juices.

Before you know it, you're living in a funhouse mirror, surrounded by amplified versions of your insecurities. Social media isn't just a window; it's a magnifying glass, zeroed in on everything you think you're lacking.

And you never even left your couch.

## Why It Feels So Personal

Let's pull back the curtain for a moment and go inside your brain.

Social comparison, according to neuroscience, lights up the same neural regions as physical pain. Yes, you read that right: seeing someone else's "success" can literally *hurt*. Your brain's threat-detection system—the amygdala—flares up, especially when you see someone with what you desire: beauty, wealth, ease, approval, stability, love.

And then, the dopamine reward system kicks in. Every like, every follow, every comment is a tiny chemical hit—a microdose of validation. This turns your emotional compass into a weather vane spinning in the digital wind. When your post gets love, you feel a high. When it's ignored, or you see someone else "winning," your mood plummets.

Here's the kicker: *even when you know it's curated— even when you intellectually understand that it's not the full picture—your body still reacts like it's real*. You watch her Bali vacation stories while sitting in traffic, and your nervous system gets the message: "She's winning. I'm stuck. Something's wrong with me."

That's not weakness. That's neurology.
So, the solution isn't to scold yourself for caring, or to try to "just get over it." The solution is to consciously retrain your system to recognize what's real and what's not.

## The "It's Just a Highlight Reel" Myth

Raise your hand if you've ever tried to soothe yourself with, "It's just a highlight reel, not the whole story!"
It's true—and it helps, sometimes. But the brain doesn't always listen. Because the truth is, you don't see the fight she had with her partner, or the anxiety attack before the speaking gig, or the existential dread she felt after her "perfect" post. You see the curated, the cropped, the filtered.

35

And even though you know this, you still feel the ache. Because your nervous system isn't rational. It's ancient. It sees status, belonging, and approval as the difference between safety and exile.

## The Hidden Cost of Constant Exposure

Let's talk about what all this scrolling actually costs us. Because it's not just "a few wasted minutes." It's so much more. Every time you open an app and scroll through a feed filled with curated perfection, you are exposing your mind to non-stop comparison triggers.

And the cost? It adds up.

- **You forget what your own voice sounds like.**
  Your opinions, desires, and dreams get drowned out by the noise of what's trending, what's viral, what's "in." Your truth starts to sound like someone else's echo.
- **You abandon creative ideas because "someone's already doing it better."**
  You had a spark—a poem, a recipe, a business idea—but then you saw someone else's version, all

polished and perfect. Suddenly, yours feels silly, so you don't bother.

- **You dress, speak, eat, post, and dream like a watered-down version of someone else.**
  You swap out your own weirdness for what's popular, what's safe, what's "likeable." You edit your existence to match a trend and call it authenticity.

- **You lose joy in the small things, because your life doesn't feel "big enough" to matter.**
  That walk you took? Not Instagrammable. The way you laughed with your friend? Too ordinary for a post. Your life starts to feel invisible.

- **You begin to edit your existence to match a trend—and call it authenticity.**
  You know that "authentic" post you spent ten minutes editing? Yeah. We've all been there.

Comparison via social media doesn't just bruise your self-esteem.

It robs you of the texture of your own life.

# The "Authenticity Trap"

Let's talk about the word "authenticity." Social media loves to preach it. "Show up as your real self! Be raw! Be vulnerable!" And yet, even authenticity gets a filter. We curate our vulnerability, softening the edges to make it palatable, likable, safe.

But here's the secret: real authenticity is messy. It's inconsistent. It's unplanned. It doesn't always look good in a grid.

If you've ever hesitated to post something real because it didn't fit the aesthetic, you know what I mean. If you've ever deleted a story because it didn't get enough views, you've felt the authenticity trap.

## Reflection Break: Digital Detox Check-In

Let's pause for a moment of radical honesty. No shame, just truth. Grab your journal, your phone's notes app, or just sit with these questions:

1. **What's the first emotion I feel after scrolling—energized, numb, inspired,**

**inferior?**

Don't overthink it. What's the vibe in your body when you close the app?

2. **Who or what am I most triggered by online? What does that say about what I think I lack?**

Is it the fitness coach? The entrepreneur? The friend with the seemingly perfect marriage?

3. **How much of my online presence is curated to avoid judgment or appear successful?**

What do you post? What do you hide? What do you delete?

4. **What would change in my body, my mood, or my day if I took a full break from comparison-based scrolling?**

Imagine it. More time? More peace? More creativity? How would your nervous system feel?

Now write this reminder where you'll see it:

"I am not behind.

I am not failing.

I am not someone else's version of success.

I am allowed to be present in my life instead of just consuming everyone else's."

## Mini Detox Practice: Curate Your Comparison

Let's build a new habit. This week, try a comparison-conscious scroll. Here's how:

- **Unfollow or mute anyone who consistently triggers your self-doubt.**
  Even if they're "nice." Even if they're "successful." You don't have to explain it. Protect your peace.
- **Follow people who normalize mess, slowness, softness, and realness.**
  Find the accounts that make you exhale, not tense up. Fill your feed with diversity, with imperfection, with the beauty of ordinary life.
- **Create before you consume.**
  Before checking feeds, write a few lines, stretch, breathe, speak out loud what you are feeling. Make something—anything—before you scroll.

- **Set a scroll timer. Boundaries = freedom.**
  Give yourself a window. When the time's up, walk away. Notice how different your day feels.

And if you feel the urge to post for approval?

Pause. Ask yourself:
"Is this expression—or is this a performance I hope earns me worth?"
If it's performance, you can still post. But at least you're doing it consciously. And that? That's the beginning of power.

## The Joy of Missing Out (JOMO)

Here's a radical idea: What if you missed out on someone else's moment—and didn't feel bad about it? What if you let yourself be out of the loop, blissfully unaware of the latest viral thing? What if you sank into your own life, your own rhythm, your own enoughness?

JOMO, the joy of missing out, is the antidote to the scroll spiral. It's presence, not performance. It's the deep satisfaction that comes from being *here*, not there. From living, not just watching.

# Final Word: You're Already Enough

You don't have to disappear into the feed.
You don't have to perform your life like it's content.
You don't have to measure your joy against someone else's projection.
You can be here. In your breath. In your moment. In your real life.

It's already enough.

And the next time you feel the urge to scroll for answers, remember:
The only mirror that matters is the one that reflects your own joy back to you.

# ✦Chapter 3✦

## The Myth of Falling Behind

*Who Told You Life Was a Race—and Why It's Time to Burn the Map*

You wake up one morning and, before your feet even hit the floor, there it is:

That quiet, persistent whisper—"I should be further along by now."

Further along where?

According to whom?

Based on what cosmic checklist?

There's no loud voice yelling, "You're late!" Just a low, anxious hum that trails you through your day—nudging you when you open LinkedIn and see yet another humblebrag post, when a friend buys a house with a kitchen island the size of your first apartment, when someone younger launches their second business, or when an old classmate is off climbing literal and metaphorical mountains while you're... just trying to keep your plants alive.

This is the chronic ache of not measuring up to a timeline you never signed up for. It's the pressure to keep up with a parade you didn't even know you joined. Spoiler: You're not lazy, failing, or broken. You're just living under a myth so deeply woven into our culture, it feels like gravity—the myth of falling behind.

But here's the truth:
There is no such thing as "behind."
Behind what? Behind whom?
Who gets to decide where the starting line is, or what "ahead" even means?

Let's take this myth and hold it up to the light. Because it's time to burn the map and build a life that fits your soul, not someone else's highlight reel.

## The Manufactured Timeline

Let's dissect the origin story of this timeline obsession. From the time you're old enough to color inside the lines, you're handed an invisible map:

- Learn this by that age.
- Look like this by then.

- Graduate by 18.
- Get a "real" job by 22.
- Partner up by 25.
- Have a baby by 30.
- Buy a house (with a white picket fence, obviously).
- Be wildly successful—but humble, glowing—but grounded, productive—but also totally rested and zen.
- And if you deviate from the schedule?
  You're behind.
  If you pause to heal, grieve, explore, or rest?
  You're wasting time.

Here's the kicker: That map was written by systems that never factored in your actual story, your trauma, your dreams, your neurodivergence, your values, your struggles, your culture, or the wild, unpredictable magic of being alive. It's a one-size-fits-none approach.

So when you panic because your life doesn't look like hers, it's not truth—it's conditioning.
It's the water we swim in, invisible but everywhere.

# Timeline Triggers

Let's get specific. Here's where the "I'm behind" myth loves to rear its head:

- **Careers:** Someone gets promoted, or makes a "30 Under 30" list. Your LinkedIn feed is a highlight reel of job changes and "so grateful for my amazing new opportunity!" posts.
- **Relationships:** Engagements, anniversaries, pregnancy announcements. Each one a reminder of where you "should" be.
- **Homes:** That moment when your friends start posting house keys and "just closed!" selfies, and you're googling "how to hang curtains without drilling holes in rental."
- **Milestones:** Travel, children, degrees, awards. There's always someone doing something you haven't done yet.
- **Healing:** Even self-growth becomes a race. "She's so much more zen than I am. Why haven't I outgrown my issues?"

Sound familiar? That's the manufactured timeline at work.

# The Loop of Never Enough

Here's how the timeline myth keeps you stuck, exhausted, and always grasping for more:

1. **You feel behind.**
   It starts as that quiet hum.
2. **You panic and overfunction—forcing growth that isn't real.**
   You sign up for courses you don't care about, say yes to things that drain you, or hustle to "catch up."
3. **You burn out or feel fake.**
   Because you're sprinting on someone else's track, not your own.
4. **You compare again.**
   The cycle restarts.
5. **You feel even more behind.**
   Because, guess what, the finish line keeps moving.

It's not that you're falling behind.
It's that you're stuck in a loop powered by someone else's milestones.

You weren't born to follow a schedule.
You were born to unfold—on your own time.

## The Comparison Trap in Action

Let's imagine:
You're having an okay day. You made your bed, watered your plants, maybe even meditated. Then, mid-scroll, you see someone your age (or, let's be honest, younger) launching a company, getting married, running a marathon, or "finally" buying a home.

Suddenly, your small victories shrink. You start mentally recalculating your "progress." You wonder if you missed the boat. You feel the urge to do more, be more, keep up— never mind that ten minutes ago you were content.

That's the timeline myth at work, turning your present into a problem to be solved, instead of a life to be lived.

## What "Late" Really Means

Let's get existential for a moment:
Late to what?
Whose party?

Who is handing out the gold stars, the "you did it right" medals, the Ultimate Adulting Award?

(If you find that committee, let me know.)

The truth is, there is no race. No final grade. No universal finish line. No judge handing out trophies at 35 or 50 or 82. You're not on pause. You're not behind. You're becoming. And sometimes, that becoming includes:

- Lost years
- Healing seasons
- Detours
- Grief
- Stuckness
- Massive pivots
- Unlearning everything you were taught

That's not failure. That's growth nobody claps for—and it's just as sacred. In fact, those "off-script" years are often where the real magic happens: the rediscovering, the deepening, the becoming.

## A Real-Life Reframe

Consider the stories that move you most—your favorite books, movies, or people. Are they the ones who followed a straight, predictable path? Or are they the ones who wandered, doubted, fell down, started over, or bloomed on a timeline nobody expected?

The most beautiful stories rarely follow a predictable arc.

# Practical Tips: How to Burn the Map (Without Burning Out)

Ready to stop living by a schedule that was never yours? Here's how to start:

## 1. Audit Your "Shoulds"

Make a list of all the timelines and "shoulds" haunting your brain:

- "I should be married by 30."
- "I should own a home by 35."
- "I should have found my purpose."
- "I should be more healed/fit/successful/confident by now."

Now, for each one, ask:

- Whose voice is this? Is it mine? My family? Culture? Instagram?
- Is this timeline even possible or healthy for me?
- Does it reflect my actual desires or just someone else's expectations?

## 2. Create a "Soul Timeline"

Instead of a checklist, write a "soul timeline":

- What do I want to learn, experience, or savor— regardless of when it happens?
- What would my milestones be if I wrote them myself?
- What are the detours I'm grateful for? What did they teach me?

## 3. Practice Timeline Detox Days

Designate a "timeline detox day" once a week. On these days:

- No social media or LinkedIn scrolls.
- No comparing your path to anyone else's.

- Focus on what feels good that day—rest, play, creating, connecting.
- Give yourself permission to be "behind" (which is really just... here).

## 4. Celebrate Unseen Growth

Start a "growth nobody claps for" journal. Write down the invisible victories:

- Boundaries you set.
- Days you rested instead of hustling.
- Lessons learned from so-called "failures."
- Moments of self-compassion.

## 5. Find Expanders, Not Competitors

Surround yourself (online and off) with people who celebrate many different timelines.
Seek out stories of late-bloomers, second-career starters, people who pivoted, paused, or flourished "off-schedule." Let their stories expand your sense of what's possible, not shrink it.

## 6. Anchor in the Present

Whenever you feel the "I'm behind" panic, come back to right now:

- What can I savor here?
- What's one thing I'm proud of today?
- What would I choose if I weren't measuring against anyone else?

## Reflection Break: Who Gave You the Clock?

Let's pause and do a timeline audit. Gently. No shame, just curiosity.

1. Where do I feel "behind"?
2. Whose voice is that—really? Family? Culture? Industry? Inner critic?
3. What timeline have I been secretly holding myself to?
4. What would my life feel like without that deadline looming over me?
5. What pace actually feels nourishing, sustainable, and aligned with who I am?

Now write this somewhere visible:

"I am not late.

I am not off course.

I am on my path.

And it's unfolding right on time."

## Mini Detox Practice: Burn the Invisible Schedule

Try this simple but potent practice:

1. Write down every timeline you've been holding yourself to.
   - "I should be married by…"
   - "I should own a home by…"
   - "I should have kids before…"
   - "I should be successful by…"
   - "I should be more healed by…"
2. Cross them out—dramatically. Burn the list if you need to. Rip it up with flair.
3. Underneath the ashes or scraps, write one question:
   - "What would my life look like if I let it be mine?"

Sit with the answer. Let it speak louder than the world.

# Bonus Practice: "Late Bloomers" List

Make a list of people you admire who bloomed "late" or on their own timeline.

- Oprah didn't get her talk show until her 30s.
- Vera Wang started designing wedding dresses at 40.
- Colonel Sanders was in his 60s when KFC took off.
- Your neighbor who went back to school at 50.
  Let their examples remind you: real timelines are wild, winding, and totally unique.

# Permission Slip: You Are Your Own Clock

You were never behind.
You were becoming on your own timeline.
And the most beautiful stories rarely follow a predictable arc.

This isn't a race.
This is a remembering.

And you, love, are right on time.

# ✦Chapter 4✦

## The Comparison Archetypes

*Meet the Inner Cast of Characters That Keep You Feeling Less Than*

Let's be real: If your mind was a reality show, the casting director would be a genius.

There's a whole inner cast—each with their own quirks, catchphrases, and drama—popping up the moment comparison creeps in. You know them: That Greek chorus of voices, personas, and energies that whisper (or sometimes shout) just loud enough to throw you off course. One minute, you're enjoying your coffee, feeling pretty good. The next, you're in a mental cage match with your own insecurities after seeing someone else thrive on your feed.

We all have them. These inner archetypes show up like well-meaning life coaches, but in reality? They're just insecure roommates with megaphones and questionable advice. They love to offer "constructive criticism," but their real specialty is keeping you stuck in the loop of comparison, self-doubt, and "never enough."

Here's the plot twist: These parts aren't inherently bad. In fact, they formed to protect you—usually way back when life was a little harsher and you needed to fit in, keep up, or stay safe. But left unchecked, they'll run the show for decades, keeping you circling the same tired story: "Why not me?"

So let's meet them. Name them. Understand them. And then gently—but firmly—ask them to step aside. Because you, love, are the only one holding the pen now.

## Archetype 1: The Shadow Twin

Meet your internal doppelgänger—the "better version of you" who always seems to be winning, glowing, and living the life you just can't quite reach. The Shadow Twin shows up when you see someone who feels eerily similar to you: same age, same background, maybe even same interests or career field—but with a shinier, more filtered existence.

She has the career you wanted.
The body you've been trying to "earn."
The lifestyle you've vision-boarded.

The relationship that looks like it came with its own Pinterest board.

And here's the kicker: You don't even hate her. In fact, you want to be her. You start taking notes. You quietly try to morph into her—adopting her routines, chasing her milestones, measuring your joy against hers. Inevitably, you end up feeling like you're failing by comparison.

**Shadow Twin Lie:**
"If I was more disciplined/magnetic/brilliant like her, I'd have what she has."

**Shadow Twin Truth:**
She is not you. You are not her. Your lives were never meant to mirror each other—and your joy doesn't need to match someone else's for it to be real.

**Practical Tip: The "Shadow Twin Inventory"**

When you notice this archetype taking over:

1. Write down what you admire or envy in your Shadow Twin.
2. Ask, "Which of these are actually meaningful to me, and which are just shiny distractions?"

3. Reclaim your own desires. What's true for YOU, not just what looks good online?

## Archetype 2: The Benchmark Babe

This is your inner ruler, the milestone-obsessed timekeeper who turns other people's timelines into your deadlines.

She's the one who whispers, "Look, she launched a business at 28! She's married with kids! Your friend just bought a house! Why are you so far behind?"

Benchmark Babe isn't even interested in whether you *want* those things. Her primary obsession is being "on track," checking boxes, and winning at the invisible game of life. She's your inner performance coordinator—and let's be honest, she's exhausting.

**Benchmark Babe Lie:**

"You should be doing more. Look at them—what's your excuse?"

**Benchmark Babe Truth:**

Someone else's pace is not your emergency. You are allowed to unfold without performing progress.

**Practical Tip: The "Benchmark Detox"**

1. Make a list of milestones you feel pressured to hit.
2. For each, ask: "Do I actually want this, or do I just feel like I should?"
3. Write yourself a permission slip: "I am allowed to unfold at my own pace. I am not on anyone else's clock."

# Archetype 3: The Inner Competitor

This one's sneaky. The Inner Competitor can turn even healing or self-growth into a race. You see someone else growing, glowing, or winning, and your stomach clenches. You didn't even know you were in competition, but suddenly, you feel less evolved, less visible, less worthy.

She'll celebrate other people's wins out loud—she's gracious, after all—but privately, she shrinks. She's the reason you hide your own wins or overanalyze theirs. She wants you to succeed, sure, but she wants you to do it faster.

**Inner Competitor Lie:**

"There's not enough room for both of us to win."

**Inner Competitor Truth:**

Someone else's light doesn't dim yours. The sky has always held room for every star to shine.

**Practical Tip: Star Map Celebration**

1. When you notice envy or competition, choose to celebrate someone else—out loud or in writing.
2. Then, list three ways your own unique "light" shines. (Hint: It doesn't have to be public or flashy.)
3. Remind yourself: "There is room for all of us. My success isn't threatened by hers."

# Archetype 4: The Invisible Self

This archetype doesn't compare out loud. She disappears the moment someone else shines. You see someone else doing something bold, beautiful, or brave, and instead of rising, you retreat. You ghost your own ideas. You shrink your presence. You convince yourself that your story's already been told—better, louder, younger, thinner, smarter, cooler.

The Invisible Self is heartbreakingly tender. She's not trying to compete or outperform. She just doesn't believe she belongs.

**Invisible Self Lie:**

"There's no room for me. I've already been outdone."

**Invisible Self Truth:**

You're not here to be original—you're here to be true. Your voice is needed, not because it's new, but because it's yours.

**Practical Tip: "I Belong Because I'm Here" Mantra**

1. Write down a list of times you felt invisible, and what triggered it.
2. For each, write a counter truth: "I belong in this space, simply because I am here."
3. Practice sharing one small thing—an idea, a story, a meal, a selfie—without editing for perfection or originality.

# The Secret Fifth Archetype: The Critic in Disguise

You know her. She's the one who says, "You're just jealous," or, "If you were better, you'd have what they have."

This archetype is a mash-up of all the others, and her favorite hobby is shaming you for even having comparison thoughts in the first place.

She's trying to keep you safe by pushing you to "improve," but really, she's just reinforcing the cycle.

**Critic Lie:**

"Comparison means you're weak or petty."

**Critic Truth:**

Comparison means you're human. Noticing it is the first step to freedom.

**Practical Tip: Compassionate Call-Out**

1. When the Critic pipes up, pause and say, "Thanks for trying to help, but I'm allowed to be human."
2. Offer yourself a small act of self-kindness—rest, a walk, a pep talk—just as you would for a friend.

63

# Reflection Break: Who's Running the Show?

Let's get honest.

1. Which of these archetypes do I hear most often?
2. What's her tone? Her script? Her favorite trigger?
3. How does she protect me—and how does she hold me back?
4. What might change in my life if I didn't believe her anymore?

Now write this, somewhere you'll see it:

"I hear you. I see you. I understand why you show up.
But I no longer let comparison lead.
I am writing a different story now—and I'm the only one holding the pen."

# Mini Detox Practice: Speak Back with Clarity

This week, when one of these archetypes shows up, try this:

1.  **Name her.** ("Ah, there's Benchmark Babe again.")
2.  **Thank her for trying to help.** ("I know you think this pressure will keep me safe.")
3.  **Speak your truth aloud.** ("But I'm allowed to go at my own pace. I don't need to match anyone.")

Say it out loud. Into the mirror. Into the moment. Into your nervous system.

## Extra Practice: Create Your "Comparison Cast" Cards

Make index cards or a note on your phone for each archetype:

- Name
- Favorite phrase
- What she's trying to protect
- The truth you want her to hear

Carry them with you. When comparison strikes, grab your card, read your truth, and breathe.

# Final Word: You're the Author Now

Detoxing comparison isn't about silencing these parts—
it's about reminding them who's in charge now.
They're allowed a seat in the room, but they don't get to
drive the car.
You're the author, the director, and the main character of
this story.

So next time the inner cast gets rowdy, remember:
You decide whose voice gets the final word.

And that, love, is where your freedom begins.

# ✦Chapter 5✦

## From Jealousy to Clarity

*How Envy Can Reveal What You Really Want—
If You're Brave Enough to Listen*

Let's have an honest moment—right here, in the no-judgment zone. Jealousy gets a bad rap. It's the emotional equivalent of spinach in your teeth: embarrassing, unsightly, and something you hope nobody notices. We treat it like a character flaw, a shameful little gremlin to be hidden under layers of spiritual concealer. We bury it in forced affirmations. We drown it in gratitude lists. We "good vibes only" ourselves into denial, shaming the feeling right out of existence.

You know the script:

- "You should be happy for her."
- "It's not a competition."
- "Good vibes only."
- "Jealousy is a low vibration."

And, sure, it can feel low. The stomach-drop, the tightness in your chest, the rush of heat to your cheeks when someone else gets the win you wanted, or seems to move through life with an ease you can't quite muster. But let's get brutally honest: just because it feels uncomfortable doesn't mean it's useless.

What if jealousy isn't your enemy?
What if it's a messenger?
What if the ache you feel when you see someone else living your "dream life" isn't a character defect—but a compass?
A cracked-open window into your deepest, most honest desires?

This chapter is your permission slip to stop judging jealousy and start decoding it. Not because you want to become a petty green monster, but because you're ready to get clear, honest, and wildly specific about what you want.

## The Truth About Jealousy

Let's define it properly. Jealousy is the discomfort that arises when you believe someone else has something you can't have. It's a comparison, but with a pinch of resentment, a dash of grief, and a whole lot of longing underneath the surface. It's not just, "She's got that, and I don't." It's, "She's allowed to have that... and somewhere, I decided I wasn't."

Oof.

That's a gut punch, right? But it's also the beginning of freedom. Jealousy isn't weakness. It's information. It's data. It's your soul's way of grabbing you by the shoulders and saying, "Hey, look—this matters to you."

And here's a plot twist: jealousy often reveals exactly where you feel disqualified from the very things your soul craves. That's not a failing. That's your inner compass, trying to get your attention.

## Why You Feel Jealous of People You Like

Let's address the confusion: Why do you feel jealous of people you adore? You're happy for her, you swear. You cheer her on. You leave supportive comments. You love her. And still... there's that little ping. That stomach drop when she shares her win. That quiet inner slump when her business goes viral, or her art gets featured, or she walks into a room with a kind of effortless presence while you're still checking if your deodorant worked.

Are you a bad person? Absolutely not. You're just being touched—by a version of you that hasn't been fully expressed yet. The jealousy isn't about her. It's about the unlived parts of you.

In fact, the closer someone is to your own values, dreams, or path, the more likely you are to feel the twinge. It's not a sign of malice. It's a sign of resonance.

## Jealousy as a Mirror

Let's reframe jealousy as a mirror, not a measurement. Instead of thinking, "She's better than me," try, "She's reflecting something I deeply want and haven't claimed yet."

When jealousy flares, get curious:

- What specifically am I reacting to?
- Is it her success? Or her confidence?
- Is it the thing she achieved—or the way she owns it?
- Do I want what she has... or how she seems to feel?

Often, it's not about the thing at all. It's about the experience you imagine it will bring:

- Freedom
- Safety
- Expression
- Celebration
- Visibility
- Permission

Jealousy shows you where your hunger lives. And you, my dear, deserve to have your hunger fed.

**Practical Tip: The Envy Inventory**

1. Next time you feel a jealous pang, write down exactly what triggered it.
2. Ask yourself, "What do I believe this person's life gives them that I'm missing?"
3. Name the core desire underneath: Is it recognition? Adventure? Creative freedom? Deep love? The right to rest?
4. Circle the feeling, not just the object. This will help you see what your soul is actually craving.

# When Jealousy Gets Loud, Get Curious

Here's your new protocol. The next time you feel that pang, pause. Instead of spiraling into shame or faking positivity, try this:

## 1. Name it.
Say it out loud or write it down: "Oof. I'm feeling jealous. Something here matters."

## 2. Drop into your body.
Where does the jealousy live? Chest? Gut? Throat? Is it hot, tight, fluttery, heavy? Stay with the sensation, not the story. Breathe into it.

## 3. Ask it:

- "What are you trying to tell me?"
- "What does she have that I'm craving?"
- "What feels possible for her but not for me?"

## 4. Then ask the real question:
"What am I ready to want out loud?"

Let your jealousy make you honest. Let it guide you to clarity. That's the detox. That's the gift.

**Practical Tip: Jealousy as a Vision Board**

Start a "Jealousy Journal."

- Each time you feel envy, jot it down.
- Next to it, write what it's showing you about your own desires.
- Use these entries as a living, breathing vision board—one built not on Pinterest fantasies, but on real, raw longing.

# Why You Don't Have to "Mute" Your Way to Peace

You don't have to unfollow or mute everyone who triggers you (though you *can* if their presence is toxic). Sometimes, the people who stir up envy are also the people who inspire us to expand, to see what's possible, to admit our own dreams without shame.

The goal isn't to eliminate all triggers. The goal is to use them as invitations—to get more honest, more clear, more aligned with what you actually want.

# The Difference Between Inspiration and Expansion

Not every jealous pang is a sign you want the *exact* thing she has. Sometimes, it's about being expanded—seeing proof that something is possible for someone like you, and letting that spark your own permission.

If you feel a twinge when someone else travels the world, maybe you don't want to backpack through Peru—but you do want more adventure, freedom, or spontaneity. If you envy a friend's creative career, maybe you want to claim your own creativity, even if it looks nothing like hers.

## Turning Jealousy into Clarity: A Step-By-Step Practice

Let's turn that envy into a roadmap, not a roadblock. Here's your step-by-step:

### 1. Spot It Without Shame

When jealousy flares, don't judge it. Name it. "I'm feeling jealous. This is just information."

## 2. Get Specific

Pinpoint the exact trigger. Was it her book launch? Her self-confidence? Her relationship? Her ability to rest without guilt?

## 3. Unpack the Story

Ask:

- "What story am I telling myself about her and about me?"
- "Where did I start believing this isn't available to me?"

## 4. Name the Desire

What do you truly want? Not in comparison to her, but for yourself—freedom, recognition, adventure, self-expression, rest, love?

## 5. Claim It Out Loud

Write it, say it, declare it: "I want _____."

## 6. Take One Tiny Aligned Action

What's one small, brave step you can take toward this desire this week? Send an email, sign up for a class, ask for what you want, take a nap, write a poem, wear the bold lipstick.

## Bonus: The "Envy to Action" Ritual

Each night, review your day. For every moment of jealousy, write:

- "I felt jealous when _____."
- "Because I want _____."
- "And I'm allowed to have it, too."

Even if you don't know how. Even if it feels light-years away. This is your declaration of possibility.

## Reflection Break: Decode the Envy

Journal time. No shame. No editing.

1. Who am I currently feeling jealous of? (Yes, name names.)
2. What exactly do I believe they have that I don't?
3. What story have I attached to their success that I've denied myself?

4. What would it look like to claim that same thing for myself—in my own way?
5. What action (even small) can I take this week to honor that desire?

Now write this declaration somewhere you'll see it:

"I am allowed to want what I want.
I am allowed to be expanded by others instead of diminished by them.
I am not behind—I'm just awakening to my own desire."

## Mini Detox Practice: Turn Envy Into Alignment

Every time you feel a pang of jealousy, write it down. One sentence:

- "I felt jealous when _____."
- "Because I want _____."
- "And I'm allowed to have it, too."

Even if you don't know how. Even if it feels far away. This is your declaration of possibility. Not because you're entitled—but because you're done pretending you don't want.

**Practical Tip: Find Your "Expanders"**

- Seek out people who live in ways that light up your own desire.
- Instead of shrinking, let their stories expand your sense of what's possible for you.
- Reach out, ask questions, connect. Most people love to share how they got where they are.
- Remember: If you can see the possibility, you can start moving toward it.

# Final Word: Permission to Want

You don't need to mute everyone who triggers you.
You don't need to spiritualize your shame.
You don't need to smile through gritted teeth when someone else wins.

You just need to stop assuming your desires are unrealistic—and start realizing they're sacred.
Because the moment you stop judging your jealousy?

It becomes the clearest map to the life you're meant to build.

So claim your wants.

Let your jealousy be your teacher, not your jailer.

And remember: You are allowed to want what you want.

# ✦Chapter 6✦

## The Body Isn't the Battlefield

*How to Reclaim Yourself from Image Obsession, Body Envy, and the Comparison Curse*

There is a quiet, nearly invisible moment that repeats itself in the lives of almost everyone raised in modern culture. You know the one. You see a picture—maybe on your feed, maybe in a group text, maybe in a random memory notification—and feel your spine cave in just a little. It's a micro-collapse, so habitual you might not notice it.

You hold your breath.

You suck in your stomach.

You untag yourself from the photo, or crop your arms, or delete the whole thing.

You change your outfit.

You whisper something cruel under your breath—aimed not at some distant foe, but at your own thighs, your skin, your face, your age, your reflection in the grocery store window.

The worst part?

It all feels so... normal.

That low hum of body comparison, that internal tug-of-war between wanting to accept yourself and the relentless urge to surveil, critique, adjust, edit, measure, hide, or fix. It's so routine, so woven into daily life, that you might not even recognize it as suffering. But it is.

This chapter is not another pep talk about "self-love" with a pastel hashtag and a green smoothie.

This is a reckoning.

A reclamation.

A relief.

Because your body was never the problem.

The culture that taught you to hate and doubt it?

That's the real thief.

## When Your Body Becomes a Scorecard

We're not born judging our bodies. We're born inhabiting them.

As children, we run, climb, get dirty, wiggle, dance in our underwear, laugh with our bellies. We eat when we're

hungry, rest when we're tired.
We live *in* our bodies.

But somewhere along the line—usually around the time someone else made a comment about your weight, your shape, your acne, your clothes, your stretch marks, your thighs, your chest, your hair—you got the memo:
"You are being looked at. And you must manage how you're seen."

From there, your body stopped being a home.
It became a project.
Something to be managed. Shrunk. Controlled. Praised. Corrected. Hidden. Sexualized. Judged. Improved. Displayed. Punished. Or "earned."

And the kicker? Even when you hit the goal weight, change your hair, buy the outfit, tone the muscle, whiten the teeth—you still feel... off. Insecure. Distracted. Not quite there yet.

That's not vanity.
That's comparison-induced dysmorphia.
It's the feeling that your real, living, breathing body is a problem to be solved—never a presence to be cherished.

## The Body as Social Capital

Let's zoom out for a second.

Your body is the most visible part of your identity. It's where all the expectations collide—beauty, femininity, masculinity, desirability, youth, health, success.

And social media? It's turned your body into an avatar—a profile image, a grid, a "before" and "after," a brand asset, a source of likes.

You're not just living in your body—you're performing it. You absorb filtered faces, impossible waistlines, post-baby abs, age-defying skin, and somehow feel like your natural human form is unacceptable by default.

You didn't choose this system.

But you've been breathing its air for so long, it feels like the truth.

It's not.

## The Scroll Spiral and Body Shame

Let's break down what happens in 0.3 seconds on the scroll spiral:

- You see her: perfect lighting, perfect skin, perfect something.
- Your brain registers lack: "I don't look like that."
- You interpret that as meaning something about your worth.
- You promise to "do better" tomorrow.
- You feel like garbage.

You forget the angle, the editing, the filters, the money, the time, the genetics, the fact that it's a curated image on a performance platform.
And you turn your real, living, breathing body into a problem—again.

That's not a flaw in you.
That's conditioning.
And it's time to cut the cord.

## Why Body Comparison Feels So Personal

Body comparison isn't just about vanity. It's about survival and social belonging. For most of human history, being accepted by the group meant safety. The rules have changed, but our brains haven't. Now, the "group" is global, and the standards are impossible.

Your body is the first thing others see—and the first thing you're taught to control, apologize for, or commodify.
If you grew up female, or queer, or in a body outside the dominant beauty norm? The pressure multiplies.
If you grew up in diet culture (spoiler: almost all of us did), you're taught to see your body as a never-ending project—always "before," never "after."

And with every scroll, every ad, every "transformation" post, the myth deepens:
Your body is your value.
Your appearance is your worth.
Your imperfections are liabilities.

But here's the secret:
Your body was never meant to be a billboard for other people's approval.

## The Cost of Body Comparison

Let's get real about what body comparison actually costs:

- **Time:** How many hours have you spent researching diets, workouts, "miracle" products, or skincare routines?

- **Money:** How much have you spent trying to chase an ever-shifting ideal?
- **Presence:** How many moments have you missed—beach days, parties, even sex—because you were fixated on how you looked?
- **Joy:** How many memories are blotted out by "I'll do it when I look better"?
- **Self-Trust:** How often do you ignore your hunger, your exhaustion, your intuition because you're trying to "earn" your worthiness?

The cost is real.

But so is your power to reclaim it.

## Practical Reclamation: Coming Home to Your Body

Ready to reclaim your body as a home, not a project? Here's how:

### 1. Unfollow to Reinhabit

**Do this today:**

- Unfollow or mute any account (yes, even the "fitspo" or "wellness" ones) that triggers body surveillance or shame—even if it's "aspirational."

- Follow people who show up in real, diverse, aging, soft, strong, vulnerable, unfiltered bodies. Fill your feed with the spectrum of humanity, not just the airbrushed highlight reel.

## 2. Stand in the Mirror—To Witness, Not Fix

- Stand in front of the mirror. Not to fix, but to witness.

- Look at yourself—your face, your belly, your scars, your smile.

- Say, "This is my body. This is my now. I am allowed to love her here."

- Optional (but powerful): Wear the outfit you've been saving "for when you look better." Wear it now. Walk tall. Eat the thing. Take the photo. Be seen.

## 3. Practice "Body Neutrality"

If "self-love" feels too far, try "body neutrality."

- You don't have to adore every inch of yourself to stop hating it.
- Try saying, "This is my body. She gets me through the day. I'm grateful. I don't owe anyone pretty."

## 4. Move for Joy—Not Punishment

- Dance in your living room. Stretch. Walk. Swim. Move in ways that feel good, not as penance for eating or being alive.
- Ask yourself, "How would I move if nobody was watching, and I didn't have to earn my right to exist?"

## 5. Reclaim Pleasure

- Eat the meal you crave, without negotiating with yourself.
- Rest when you're tired—not when you're "allowed."

- Wear the perfume, the red lipstick, the soft sweater.

- Let your body be a source of pleasure, not just a problem to solve.

## 6. Set Boundaries Around Body Talk

- Gently redirect conversations that spiral into diet talk or body shaming.
- If a friend or family member comments on your body, try: "I'm not focusing on my appearance right now. Can we talk about something else?"
- Protect your peace like it's sacred—because it is.

## Reflection Break: The Body as Home

Take a moment. Journal, voice note, or simply sit with these:

1. When did I first become self-conscious of my body? What moment shaped that awareness?
2. Whose body am I silently comparing mine to most often? What story am I attaching to their appearance?

3. What would it feel like to trust my body instead of critique it?

4. What have I postponed "until I look better"? What would it mean to stop waiting?

Now write this:

"I am allowed to be seen without editing myself.
I am allowed to exist without performing thinness, youth, perfection, or trendiness.
My body is not an apology—it is an instrument of presence, pleasure, and power."

## Mini Detox Practice: Body Liberation in Action

Try these for one week:

- **Unfollow to Reinhabit:** Unsubscribe from body shame—digitally and socially.

- **Mirror Ritual:** Choose one part of your body each day and name three things it lets you do.

- **Pleasure Practice:** Do one thing each day that feels good in your skin—stretching, good food, touch, rest.

- **Wear the "Someday" Outfit:** Yes, today. Not when you're "better." Now.

- **Radical Compliment:** Compliment someone (or yourself!) on something unrelated to appearance: "You make me laugh." "Your energy is magnetic." "I love how you light up a room."

## Optional Expansion: The Community of Real Bodies

Surround yourself with people who celebrate real bodies.

- Seek out communities—online or in person— where diversity of form, age, ability, and style is the standard, not the exception.
- Share your own unfiltered moments with trusted friends—let yourself be seen, and see others in return.

# Permission Slip: You Are Not Late to Your Own Acceptance

You do not need to shrink to be worthy of space.

You do not need to earn softness, slowness, sensuality, or visibility.

You are not late to your own acceptance.

## Final Word: This Body Is Home

This is your home.

This body. This moment. This breath.

And you, dear one, are allowed to live here—fully, joyfully, and without apology.

# ✦Chapter 7✦

## Creating Without Competing

*How to Reclaim Your Voice, Your Work, and Your Joy Without Looking Over Your Shoulder*

There's a unique ache that only creative souls know: the sting of watching someone else do the very thing you dreamed of doing—and feeling like you just lost before you even started.

You were on the edge. You had your poem half-finished, your business plan sketched, your camera set to record that first brave video. Your finger hovered over "post." And then... you scrolled.

Suddenly, there she was—doing it. Louder. Brighter. Smoother. With the branding, the audience, the perfect lighting, the confidence you hoped would magically appear the moment you hit "share."

In a heartbeat, your fire fizzled.

You closed the tab, tucked your idea away for "later," and whispered a silent, "Never mind."

That's the real cost of comparison.

It's not just lost joy—it's lost expression.

But here's the truth that can set you free:

Your creativity doesn't need to be the best.

It just needs to be yours.

## Why We Shrink When We Should Be Shining

Let's name the process, because awareness is the first step toward freedom:

- You see someone else succeed.
- Instead of being inspired, you feel erased.
- You think, "They've already said it, done it, claimed it."
- You start doubting your originality.
- You label your dream redundant.
- You ghost your own vision.

It's a theft that happens in silence. You convince yourself that your idea, your voice, your work isn't needed because someone else got there first.

But here's what the world doesn't tell you:
Originality was never the point.
Authenticity was.

Creativity is not about being the first, the best, or the loudest. It's about being *true*—to your voice, your story, your way of seeing.

## The "There's No Room" Myth

Comparison thrives on a lie: scarcity.
The myth that there's only room for a few to shine, that if someone else takes up space, there's less left for you.

But let's break that myth.
Imagine if musicians stopped writing love songs because someone else already had.
Imagine if painters stopped painting sunsets because Monet beat them to it.
Imagine if mothers stopped mothering because someone else already gave birth.

Art is not a race.
Creativity is not a contest.
Expression is not a zero-sum game.

You showing up doesn't take away from anyone else. It adds something to the world that only you could ever bring.

**Your work is worth doing—even if it's been done.**

## Why "Original" Is Overrated—and "True" Is Everything

Let's get honest:

Yes, someone has probably already written the thing you're thinking of writing.

Yes, someone has made a product like yours.

Yes, someone is out there doing something similar.

But they haven't done it like *you*.

With your voice.

Your story.

Your flavor.

Your magic.

Even if 100 people have said it before, your version might be the only one that lands for someone who desperately needs to hear it—at this moment, in this way, in your words.

You're not here to be the first.

You're here to be *real.*

## The Science: The Creative Brain on Comparison

Neuroscience shows us that creativity and comparison use different neural pathways.

When you're in a creative state—what researchers call "flow"—your brain's default mode network (DMN) lights up, allowing for original connections, intuition, and joy. But when you compare, your brain's social evaluation centers activate. You shift from self-expression to self-surveillance, from making to measuring.

No wonder you feel blocked.

Comparison hijacks your creativity because you can't make art and monitor your ranking at the same time.

### The fix?

Cut off the comparison at its source—at least for a while—and give yourself permission to create in a vacuum.

# The Power of Your Unique Frequency

Think of your creative voice as a radio frequency.
If you're constantly tuning in to everyone else's station, you'll never hear your own song.

Your life, your experiences, your heartbreaks, your humor, your perspective—no one else has your frequency. When you create from that place, your work vibrates with a resonance that can't be faked or replicated.

And here's a secret:
The people you admire most? They weren't first. They were just true.

# Practical Reclamation: How to Create Without Competing

Let's get you out of the comparison spiral and back into your own creative flow. Here's your roadmap:

## 1. Create Before You Consume

Start your day (or your creative session) without scrolling, researching, or "getting inspired."

Even 10 minutes of unfiltered creation can shift your energy from imitation to originality.

## 2. Set a "No-Peeking" Challenge

For the next 48 hours, create in a vacuum:

- No scrolling.
- No checking what "the competition" is up to.
- No seeing how others phrase it, style it, sing it, or sell it.
- Just make. Write. Paint. Build. Dance.
- Share something—it doesn't have to be perfect. It just has to be yours.

You'll be amazed how free your voice sounds when it's not trying to compete—just express.

## 3. Name Your Creative Triggers

Take inventory:

- Who do you compare yourself to the most?
- When does your comparison spiral get loudest? (Morning? After scrolling? When launching something new?)

- What story do you attach to their success vs. your own?

Naming your triggers helps you catch comparison before it can steal your spark.

## 4. Redefine "Success"

What if success wasn't about numbers, applause, or virality, but about the act of showing up as yourself?

- Write your own creative manifesto: "I create to feel alive. I share to connect. I make things because I'm here."

## 5. Celebrate Small Acts of Expression

Every time you share something—no matter how small—celebrate it.
Not for validation, but as an act of bravery.

## Reflection Break: Reclaiming Creative Confidence

Write freely and honestly:

1. What have I stopped myself from creating or sharing out of fear that it's not original or good enough?
2. Who am I comparing myself to creatively? What story have I made up about their success?
3. What would I create or say if I believed there was room for me?
4. What does my voice sound like when I'm not trying to mimic someone else's style or tone?

Now remind yourself:

"My voice is valid.
My art is enough.
My work belongs in the world—not because it's new, but because it's mine."

## Mini Detox Practice: Create Without Peeking

For the next 48 hours, try this experiment:

- No consuming. Don't scroll. Don't research. Don't "get inspired."

- Just create. Write. Paint. Speak. Dance. Build. Design.
- Share something. It doesn't have to be perfect. It just has to be yours.

Create in a vacuum. Not because you live there—but because you need space to hear your own voice without comparing it to someone else's frequency.

Then, when you're ready, share it. Not for applause. Not for validation. Just as an act of return.

You'll be amazed how free your voice sounds when it's not trying to compete—just express.

## Permission Slip: You Were Made to Radiate

You weren't made to replicate.
You were made to radiate.

The world doesn't need another version of someone else. It needs your truth. Your messy, beautiful, bold expression.

And it's never too late to stop hiding.

102

# ✦Chapter 8✦

## Comparison in Relationships: Love, Friendship, and the Social Scoreboard

You know that moment: you're having a perfectly decent day with your partner, your best friend, or your family. The sun is shining; your coffee is actually hot. Then—bam!—someone posts a "couple goals" reel or a group selfie from a trip you weren't invited to. Suddenly, you're not basking in the glow of your own relationships. You're spiraling into a mental PowerPoint presentation on why everyone else's love is deeper, their group texts are funnier, their friendships are more "ride or die," their family is more photogenic. Welcome to the social scoreboard: where love and friendship become spectator sports, and you're pretty sure you're losing.

Let's get real: comparison doesn't just live in your closet or your Instagram feed. It sleeps in your bed, eats at your dinner table, and sometimes even slides into your DMs. Your relationships—romantic, platonic, familial—are supposed to be sanctuaries. But when comparison gets in, even the warmest hug can feel like a consolation prize.

## Why We Compare Our Connections

First, let's get honest about why this happens. Humans are wired for belonging. Our ancestors survived by bonding, aligning, and keeping tabs on the tribe. Fast-forward a few millennia, and we're still scanning for cues that we're loved, safe, and "in." Only now, the measure isn't who shares the last berry—it's who gets tagged in the most stories, whose partner writes the gushiest anniversary post, and who gets invited to the "cool" dinner party.

This isn't shallow. It's survival—only now, connection is currency.
But here's the toxic twist: the moment you start quantifying love, you stop feeling it.

We're all walking around with invisible scoreboards—tallying who texted first, who called last, who planned the last get-together, who got the bigger birthday shoutout. It's exhausting, and it turns relationships into a series of transactions, not moments of true connection.

# Relationship FOMO: The Uninvited Guest

"Fear of Missing Out" isn't just about parties. It's that gnawing ache when you see your friends hanging out without you, your partner laughing a little too hard at someone else's joke, or your sibling's family group chat looking like a Hallmark movie while yours is... mostly memes and ghosted texts.

You start to question:
*Am I enough? Is my relationship boring? Did I peak in friendship in 2012? Why does everyone else's group chat look like a therapy session mixed with a comedy club?*

Here's the truth bomb: most of those curated moments are just that—curated.
Nobody posts the third hour of awkward small talk, the fight over who forgot to Venmo for brunch, or the couple's silent drive home after the big anniversary dinner. And that "perfect" couple? I guarantee at least one of them is considering therapy, or at least a solo vacation.

# Romantic Comparison: The "Better Half" Illusion

Comparison in love is the fastest way to kill desire, joy, and the sweet, weird intimacy that comes from presence. Maybe your partner isn't a poet. Maybe your anniversary didn't involve a helicopter ride over the Amalfi Coast. Maybe your last date night was Netflix and pizza, and you both fell asleep before the credits.

You know what? That's real. That's yours. And it's sacred.

But when you measure it against the highlight reel, you'll always come up short. You'll start resenting the person in front of you for not being someone else's fantasy.

**Comparison is the enemy of gratitude.**
It turns "enough" into "not enough."
It makes you forget the little rituals, the inside jokes, the weird shorthand that only you two understand.

# Friendship Envy: The Inner Circle Complex

You know those friend groups who seem to have matching tattoos, a group chat called "The Coven," and a highlight reel of sleepovers and brunches and coordinated costumes? Or maybe it's the "business besties" who collaborate, travel, and do trust falls in Bali, while you're just trying to get a text back.

It's easy to feel like an outsider—even in your own friendships. Here's the kicker:
Most so-called "squads" have their own drama, silent rivalries, and unspoken hierarchies.
You're not missing out—you're just not seeing the mess.

Real friendship isn't measured in selfies. It's measured in the comfort of being unfiltered, the ability to be your weird self, and the willingness to show up when things aren't pretty.

## Family Ties and Sibling Rivalry 2.0

Family comparison is the OG.
Who's the favorite? Who's doing "better"? Who's got the

most photogenic kids, the biggest house, the happiest marriage, the least baggage?

If you grew up measuring your worth against a sibling, cousin, or that one "golden child" everyone secretly resents, welcome to the club.

The family scoreboard is a trap. It keeps you stuck— forever chasing approval and missing the weird, wonderful reality of your own story.

## The Social Scoreboard: Why It Hurts

Here's why the scoreboard stings so much: it attaches your worth to metrics you can't control.

- Number of likes.
- Number of invites.
- Number of gushing public declarations.
- Number of "goals" hashtags.

But love doesn't thrive in spreadsheets. And a real connection can't be measured in public displays.

# Detox Practice: Reclaim Your Connections

Let's get practical. Here are five steps to detox from comparison in relationships and reclaim your connections:

## 1. Stop Keeping Score

If you find yourself tallying who called last, who texts first, or who posts about you most, pause. Step away from the scoreboard. Love doesn't thrive in ledgers.

## 2. Name the Good

List what's unique, quirky, and irreplaceable about your relationships. Celebrate the inside jokes, the weird traditions, the way your friend always sends you memes at 2 a.m., the way your partner knows exactly how you take your coffee.

## 3. Have the Unfiltered Conversation

Tell your people when you feel left out or when you're comparing. Vulnerability is the antidote to silent suffering. Sometimes the fastest way to dissolve shame is to name it out loud.

## 4. Choose Presence Over Performance

Next time you're with your people, put your phone away. Be in the moment. Notice how much more you laugh when you're not mentally rehearsing an Instagram caption or wondering if your selfie is "cute enough to post."

## 5. Unfollow (or Mute) the Triggers

If certain accounts, friends, or even family members consistently make you feel "less than," it's okay to take a break. Protect your energy. You're allowed to curate your digital environment for your own peace.

## Reflection Break

- Where do I most often compare my relationships?
- What do I believe other people have in their connections that I don't?
- How might my relationships deepen if I stopped measuring them against someone else's?

- What's irreplaceably real, weird, or beautiful about my own connections?

Write these answers down. Let yourself see what's true, not just what's missing.

## The Truth About Belonging

You don't need to win the friendship Olympics or the couple's costume contest.
The relationships that matter are the ones that make you feel seen, safe, and a little bit more yourself.

The rest? Let them scroll on by.

# ✦Chapter 9✦

## Reclaiming Your Own Damn Lane

*What It Means to Define Success on Your Terms—And Stay Rooted in It*

There comes a moment—usually after your fourth identity crisis of the week—when you realize the reason you're so tired isn't because you're not doing enough.

It's because you're running someone else's race.

You've been living by timelines you didn't design, chasing goals you don't care about, measuring yourself with someone else's ruler, and wondering why nothing feels right—even when, on paper, you're technically "doing well."

This is the burnout nobody talks about. The exhaustion that comes from hustling against your own nature, doing everything "right" but feeling wrong inside your own life.

This chapter is your permission slip to quit the rat race and walk your own sacred road. Not slower. Not lazier. Not safer. Just truer.

Because your joy doesn't live in "better."
It lives in *aligned*.

## The Real Reason You Feel Behind

Let's tell the truth:
You don't actually want what she has.
You want the feeling you *imagine* she has:

- Freedom
- Fulfillment
- Ease
- Belonging
- Validation
- Confidence

You see her life and think, *If I had that, I'd finally be okay.*
But even if you did have it, it still wouldn't fit. Because you weren't made for her lane. You were made for yours.

113

**Your desires, your pace, your weirdness, your rhythms, your story—they aren't obstacles. They're coordinates.**

If you keep outsourcing your path to other people's definitions of "winning," you'll keep burning out in borrowed shoes.

## The Psychology of "Lanes"

Psychologists call this "self-concordant goals"—objectives that are aligned with your true values and interests. Research shows that when your goals are truly yours (not imposed by parents, peers, or culture), you're more motivated, less anxious, and far more likely to feel fulfilled—even if your progress looks zigzaggy or slow from the outside.

## What Your Lane Actually Looks Like

Let's get clear:

Your lane isn't a brand.

It's not an aesthetic.

It's not the version of your life that performs well on Instagram.

Your lane is the rhythm of your own nervous system.

It's the relationships that nourish you, not impress others.

It's the work that brings you alive, even if no one claps for it.

It's the pace that doesn't burn you out.

It's the version of success that lets you sleep at night.

**Your lane is yours because it feels like home.**

And yes—sometimes you'll veer. You'll forget. You'll slide into the comparison ditch. That's okay.

The work isn't to stay in your lane perfectly.

It's to remember it more quickly.

To keep coming back.

## The Myth of the Upward Trajectory

Let's dismantle another myth: the idea that success should look like a straight, upward line.

Spoiler: it doesn't.

Real success is often:

- Zigzagging

- Pausing
- Redirecting
- Burning it all down and starting again
- Saying "no" to things that make you money but drain your soul
- Saying "yes" to things that make no sense but feel true

Success in your lane won't always look "successful" to the outside world.

But it will feel like *alignment*.

And that's the kind of wealth that can't be faked.

## The Power of Pivots

Every major creative, entrepreneur, or leader you admire has had to pivot, pause, or start over.

Oprah was fired from her first TV job. Vera Wang became a designer at 40.

J.K. Rowling was a single mom on welfare before Harry Potter.

Alignment often looks like failure from the outside—until it doesn't.

# The Comparison Trap: "Am I Behind?"

"Behind" is a story sold by a culture obsessed with timelines.

Graduated by X.

Get married by Y.

Hit six figures by Z.

Buy a house, have kids, retire, look happy doing it all.

But life isn't a conveyor belt.

Your lane might be slower, weirder, or more winding—and that's not a flaw.

It's a feature.

## Social Media and the Highlight Reel

Remember: social media is a museum of other people's best moments, curated and filtered to look like a straight path.

Don't compare your behind-the-scenes to someone else's highlight reel.

You're not behind. You're just on your own timeline.

# Practical Reclamation: How to Find (and Stay In) Your Lane

Let's get tactical. Here's how to anchor yourself in your own damn lane:

## 1. Sacred Lane Audit

This week, do a personal audit.
Look at how you're spending your:

- Time
- Energy
- Money
- Attention

For each area, ask:
"Is this aligned with my values? Or am I doing this to keep up, prove something, or earn validation?"

Circle what feels true. Cross out what feels performative. Then choose one small way to pivot back into your lane this week.

It could be:

- Saying no to something that drains you
- Spending time on something that nourishes you, even if it "goes nowhere"
- Changing your schedule, your wardrobe, your goals, your mind

You're allowed to reroute. As many times as it takes.

## 2. Write Your Own Success Statement

If no one ever judged you again, what would success look like for you?
Write it out, unapologetically. Maybe it reads:

"Success is waking up rested, working on creative projects, having slow breakfasts with my partner, and spending time in nature."

Or maybe:

"Success is building something meaningful, traveling solo, and making art that feels like a conversation with the world."

Let it be yours.

## 3. Name and Release the Old Rulers

Whose version of success are you unconsciously living out right now?

Parents? Influencers? Old bosses?

Name them.

Thank them for their influence—and then consciously choose what you want to keep or release.

## 4. Permission to Pivot (Again, and Again)

Give yourself permission to slow down, pivot, or choose differently without shame.

You're not a quitter for changing your mind.

You're a human being, growing and learning.

## Reflection Break: Define It for Yourself

Answer these slowly. Like you're drawing a map back to your own heart:

1. If no one ever judged me again, what would success look like for me?
2. Whose version of success am I unconsciously living out right now?

3. What part of me feels like it's "not allowed" to slow down, choose differently, or pivot?

4. What am I ready to stop chasing? What am I ready to start claiming?

And now this:

"I'm not here to be impressive.
I'm here to be aligned.
My lane may not make sense to others.
But it was never supposed to."

## Mini Detox Practice: Realignment Rituals

Try one of these each day for the next week:

- **Morning Check-In:** Before you start your day, ask, "What would feel most like me today?"
- **Aligned Action:** Choose one action that's just for you, not for applause.
- **Comparison Detox:** Limit social media, especially in the morning and evening.
- **Evening Reflection:** Ask, "Where did I honor my own lane today? Where did I slip into someone else's?"

# A New Definition of Winning

Winning isn't crossing a finish line someone else drew.
It's feeling at home in your own life—even if no one else
gets it.

You don't need to speed up to catch her.
You need to slow down to hear yourself.

You don't need to prove that you're on track.
You just need to remember: you were never off track.

Your lane doesn't have to be flashy.
It just has to be yours.

# ✦Chapter 10✦

# The Achievement Olympics: Careers, Money, and Status Anxiety

Ever notice how "So, what do you do?" is always followed by a subtle scan—are you impressive, are you busy enough, are you booked and blessed, or are you just... basic? Welcome to the Achievement Olympics, where everyone's running, jumping, and contorting themselves to win medals that no one even remembers to hand out.

Let's be honest: Career, money, and status are the last socially acceptable ways to openly compare ourselves. It's the grown-up version of "my dad can beat up your dad"— except now it's "my job title is longer than your LinkedIn bio" or "my side hustle has a side hustle."

## Hustle Culture: The Never-Ending Relay Race

In the world of perpetual striving, it's never enough to simply have a job. You need a passion. A mission. A brand. Oh, and a five-year plan. And if you're not waking up at 5 a.m. to meditate, cold plunge, journal, and send gratitude emails before breakfast—are you even trying?

Comparison at work is a slippery slope. You start by admiring someone's accomplishments, and before you know it, you're doom-scrolling job postings at 2 a.m., convinced you missed the train to "meaningful work."

## Money: The Silent Measuring Stick

No one talks about money, but everyone feels it. Salary. Savings. Home ownership. Vacation destinations. Even your dog's brand of kibble is up for comparison. The pressure to "make it" is everywhere, but the rules are always changing.

And the worst part? The more you earn, the higher the bar gets. Suddenly, "enough" is just out of reach, and someone else is always posting about their bonus, their investment property, or their minimalist yet expensive kitchen renovation.

# Status Symbols: The Comparison Currency

Let's play a game: How many status symbols can you spot in one social media scroll? Luxury handbags. Tesla deliveries. "Work from anywhere" tropical backdrops. Engagement announcements with custom calligraphy. You get the idea.

But here's the plot twist—the stuff that looks impressive rarely feels as good as you think it will. The dopamine hit fades, but the comparison hangover lingers.

## When Your Career Becomes Your Identity

Our culture loves to define people by what they do. But when your job becomes your identity, any professional wobble feels like a personal failure.

Here's the truth: Your value isn't your productivity. Your worth isn't your net worth. And your LinkedIn headline is not your legacy.

## The Status Spiral: Why "Enough" Never Feels Like Enough

125

Comparison keeps you stuck on the hamster wheel—no matter how fast you run, someone else is always ahead. You chase promotions, certifications, and "success," but the finish line keeps moving.

Spoiler alert: There is no finish line. There's just you, getting older, hopefully wiser, and (if you're lucky) realizing that the only scoreboard that matters is the one inside your own chest.

## Detox Practice: Opt Out of the Olympics

1. **Redefine Success.**
   Make a list of what actually matters to you—not your industry, your parents, or your college roommate. What would "winning" look like if nobody else was watching?

2. **Unsubscribe from Hustle Porn.**
   Mute the influencers, podcasts, and newsletters that make you feel like a slacker. Rest is resistance, and your hustle is not your worth.

3. **Talk About Money (For Real).**
   Have honest conversations with friends about finances, privilege, and what's real. The silence is where shame breeds.

4. **Celebrate Small Wins.**

   You don't need a promotion to feel proud. Did you set a boundary? Take a risk? Help someone? That's Olympic-level living.

5. **Remember: Comparison is the Thief of Joy, and Status is a Terrible God.**

   Worship at the altar of your own enoughness.

## Reflection Break

- In what areas of my work or finances do I most compare myself?
- What status symbols trigger me—and why?
- What would my career look like if I stopped measuring it against someone else's timeline?

## The Freedom of Enough

You're not here to win the Olympics. You're here to build a life that feels good on the inside, not just impressive on the outside. The real gold medal? Contentment. And babe, it's one you get to award yourself.

# ✦Chapter 11✦

# Unsubscribing from the "Better" Trap

*How to Exit the Loop of Self-Optimization and Remember You're Already Enough*

Let's be honest.

"Better" sounds innocent enough. Motivational, even. It hides in well-meaning advice, Pinterest quotes, and every second wellness reel on your feed.

"Be the best version of yourself."
"Every day, in every way, getting better and better."
"Glow up."
"Uplevel."
"Fix your mindset. Fix your life."

But under all the gloss and grit?
"Better" often translates to *"Not quite enough yet."*

This chapter is your unsubscribe form.

Not from growth, evolution, or healing.

But from the toxic illusion that you need to constantly upgrade yourself to be worthy of peace, love, belonging, or rest.

## When Self-Improvement Becomes Self-Rejection

Let's name what's really going on.

You think you're improving yourself.
But what you're actually doing is *chasing worthiness.*

You've read all the books. Done the inner work. Bought the courses. Made the vision boards. Tracked the habits. Told yourself, "Once I just _____, I'll finally feel good."

But the finish line keeps moving, doesn't it?

The body goal shifts.
The career ladder grows another rung.
The mindset needs one more tweak.
The next version of you still isn't quite there.

And somewhere, silently, you wonder:

"Is there ever going to be a version of me that's allowed to *just be*?"

That question is the beginning of liberation.

## The Psychology of Perpetual Not-Enoughness

Self-optimization plays on your brain's wiring for survival and belonging.

If your nervous system was trained to equate being "better" with being safer, more lovable, or more accepted, you'll keep seeking upgrades—because your inner child still believes love has to be earned.

So "I want to improve" quietly turns into:

"I need to fix this part of me so I can finally feel okay."

It's not just hustle culture.
It's an emotional survival strategy.

But you're not broken.
You're just *trained to think your healing has to look like constant progress.*

# When Healing Starts to Look Like Hustle

Let's get brutally honest.

You can end up doing personal growth the same way you did people-pleasing:

- Performing it
- Perfecting it
- Sharing only the palatable parts
- Shaming yourself for not being further along
- Needing others to see your evolution to believe it matters

But healing isn't about becoming impressive.

It's about becoming *free*.

You don't need another productivity hack, morning routine, or journal prompt to be valid. You need to *remember who you were before you started over-editing your soul*.

# Reflection Break: Who Are You Trying to "Better"?

Let's slow down and get real.

1. What parts of me do I keep trying to improve, even though they're already tender and worthy?
2. Where have I equated self-growth with self-correction?
3. Who am I still trying to impress with my evolution?
4. What would it feel like to rest—not because I earned it, but because I *exist*?

And now, this reminder:

"I don't need to be better to be enough.
I am allowed to grow without shaming who I am now.
I am not a project. I am a person.
And I am allowed to love myself at every draft."

# Mini Detox Practice: Opt Out of Optimization

This week, choose one area of your life where you usually strive—and intentionally do *nothing to improve it.*

Don't biohack your sleep.
Don't try to eat "clean."
Don't squeeze another productivity tip into your morning.
Don't force joy.
Don't fix your mindset.

Instead, ask:

"What if I'm okay here? As I am? In this moment?"

And let that be enough.

This isn't regression.
This is resistance.
This is radical self-trust.

Because not everything needs to be optimized.
Some things need to be *lived.*

You don't need to be "better."
You need to be *home*—in yourself, your softness, your honesty, your rhythm.

133

The version of you reading this right now?

She's already worthy of rest.
She's already worthy of love.
She's already worthy of being chosen—*without a single upgrade.*

You don't need to transform to deserve your own compassion.
You just need to *remember that you never lost it.*

# ✦Chapter 12✦
# The Comparison Trap in Parenting and Family Life

Let's get brutally honest: Parenting is already a contact sport, and comparison is the referee that nobody asked for. Whether you're a mom, dad, step-parent, "cool aunt," or you've chosen to be childfree, the family scoreboard is alive and well—and it's absolutely exhausting.

## The Mommy Wars and Dad Olympics

You know the drill: Whose kid hits milestones first? Who has the "right" stroller, preschool, or Pinterest-worthy birthday party? Who breastfeeds, who bottle-feeds, who co-sleeps, who "loses the baby weight" in record time? And don't even get started on discipline styles, screen time, or gluten.

There's a reason parenting forums are digital war zones. But here's the secret nobody posts about: Every parent feels like they're failing at something. Every. Single. One.

## The Childfree Comparison

Maybe you don't have kids—by choice, by circumstance, or by heartbreak. That doesn't exempt you from the family comparison circus. The questions, the judgments, the subtle suggestions that your life is "missing something." As if fulfillment comes in only one flavor.

You get to write your own story. And it's just as worthy—no matter how many people are on your holiday card.

## Family Dynamics: Sibling Showdowns and Generational Guilt

The family comparison trap started long before you had your own family (or didn't). Sibling rivalry, parental expectations, generational "shoulds"—it's all there, shaping your sense of enoughness.

How many times have you heard, "When are you going to settle down?" or "Your cousin just got promoted!" or "I was married with three kids by your age…" Yeah. Hard pass.

# Social Media: The Highlight Reel of Family Life

Instagram moms with perfectly coordinated outfits and toddlers who eat kale chips. Dads who build treehouses and coach soccer while running a startup. Family vacations that look like tourism board ads. It's easy to feel like your family is the blooper reel to everyone else's blockbuster.

But I promise: Behind every "perfect" family photo is a bribe, a meltdown, and at least one questionable stain.

## Parenting Your Inner Child

Comparison doesn't just show up in your actual family. It lives in your inner family—the voices you internalized, the standards you absorbed, the wounds you carry. Sometimes, you're not competing with your sister—you're competing with your childhood self, or the parent you wish you'd had.

# Detox Practice: Unfollow the Family Script

1. **No More Milestone Olympics.**
   Your kid (or your inner child) is on their own timeline. Celebrate what's real, not what's "expected."

2. **Ditch the Mom (or Dad, or Childfree) Guilt.**
   You don't owe anyone an explanation for your family choices.

3. **Have the Real Talk.**
   Share your struggles with trusted friends. Vulnerability beats silent shame every time.

4. **Curate Your Feed.**
   Mute the accounts that make you feel like you're failing at family, and follow the ones that show the mess, the joy, and the weirdness.

5. **Reparent Yourself.**
   Give yourself the compassion you wish you'd gotten growing up. You're raising yourself, too.

## Reflection Break

- Where do I most compare myself in family life?

- What scripts or expectations am I still carrying from childhood?
- What would family mean to me if I stopped measuring it against someone else's highlight reel?

## Permission to Be Enough

You don't need to win the family Olympics. You don't have to be the perfect parent, child, or sibling. You just have to be present, honest, and willing to write your own rules. Your family—by birth or by choice—is already enough. And so are you.

# ✦Chapter 13✦

## Learning to Like Your Life Again

*How to Root Into Contentment Without Settling for Less*

At the heart of comparison is this quiet, aching question: "Is my life enough?"

Not just tolerable. Not just productive. Not just technically fine.
But *enough to like*.
Enough to belong to.
Enough to want to wake up in, over and over again.

When the noise is loud, when the scroll is endless, when the world keeps dangling shinier lives and faster timelines, your own life can start to feel like a placeholder. A project. A disappointment. Maybe you find yourself thinking, "If only I could get there. If only I could fix this. If only I could be more like her, or them, or that."

But here's the thing no one tells you:
You don't have to earn your way into a life you enjoy.

You don't have to wait until it's shinier, slimmer, more stable, or more "on-brand."

You're allowed to like your life now—even if it's unfinished, weird, simple, chaotic, or deeply quiet.

You're allowed to find joy in what already belongs to you.

## Liking Isn't Settling

We live in a culture that worships hunger, hustle, and the next big thing. There's a myth that says if you're content, you must be lazy. If you like your life, you must have stopped trying. If you love what you have, you must have given up on wanting more.

But contentment isn't stagnation.
It's sovereignty.

Contentment says:
"This life is mine. I built this. I'm not waiting to live until it's better. I'm living now."

Liking your life doesn't mean it's perfect.
It means you've stopped outsourcing your joy to a future version of yourself.

That's not settling.

That's arriving.

## Contentment vs. Complacency: The Science

Research shows that people who practice gratitude and savoring—focusing on what's already good—are not less ambitious. In fact, they're more resilient and more likely to take healthy risks. When you like your life, you have a stable foundation from which to grow. You're not chasing from a place of emptiness, but building from a place of plenty.

## What Happens When You Stop Waiting

When you stop measuring your life against hers (or theirs, or the feed), something magical happens. You start to hear your own laughter again. You notice the way the sun hits your floor in the morning. You finally start that project—not for validation, but because you want to. You stop scrolling for proof you're okay. You feel safe in your skin, even when nothing dramatic is happening.

You realize that joy isn't in the "someday."

It's in the details.

And those details?

They were never small.

They were just waiting for you to look.

## The Art of Savoring

Psychologists call this "savoring"—the practice of noticing and appreciating small, positive moments as they happen. Studies show that savoring increases happiness, decreases stress, and strengthens your sense of meaning. It's not about pretending everything is perfect. It's about letting what's good be *enough* for today.

## The Courage to Like Your Life (Even If It's Unfinished)

Liking your life—even if it's not a highlight reel—can feel radical. It takes courage to say, "I'm allowed to want this. I'm allowed to love this. I'm allowed to enjoy my days, even before they're perfect."

Here's the secret:

You don't have to post about it.

You don't have to justify it.
You don't have to prove it to anyone.

Joy in the ordinary is a quiet kind of rebellion.
It's a way to take your power back from the endless scroll,
the endless striving, the endless "not yet."

## Reflection Break: What Do I Already Love?

Take this slowly. Go small, not big.

1. **What do I already love about the life I've built—quietly, secretly, without needing to prove it to anyone?**
   - Maybe it's the way your morning coffee tastes in your chipped favorite mug.
   - Maybe it's the sound of your child's laughter, or the stillness before anyone else wakes up.
   - Maybe it's the playlist you made for late-night drives, or the plant that keeps thriving on your windowsill.
2. **What do I rush past every day that actually brings me peace, pride, or pleasure?**

- o   The neighbor who always waves.
- o   The tree outside your window.
- o   The way you make your bed, or don't.

3. **Where have I been waiting for life to get "better" before letting myself feel good?**
   - o   "When I lose weight."
   - o   "When I get the promotion."
   - o   "When I move."

4. **What would it mean to say: "This life is mine. And I like it here."**
   - o   How would you show up differently?
   - o   What would you stop apologizing for?
   - o   What would you notice more?

Now write this:

"I don't have to wait until everything is fixed to love what's real.
I don't have to apologize for finding joy in the ordinary.
I am allowed to like my life before it's finished."

# Mini Detox Practice: The Enoughness Inventory

This week, take inventory—not of what needs fixing, but of what's already enough.

Make a list titled:

**"Things I Like About My Life (Even if No One Else Notices)"**

Include things like:

- The way your dog greets you.
- Your playlist for early morning drives.
- The quiet after everyone else has gone to bed.
- The way you made that one friend laugh last week.
- Your handwriting. Your favorite coffee mug. The moment you exhaled and meant it.
- The old sweater you refuse to throw away.
- That one patch of sunlight on your floor.

Don't post it. Don't edit it. Don't justify it.
Just feel it.

Let that list remind you that you're not waiting for joy to find you.

You're rediscovering it—in the life you're already living.

## Embodying Contentment: Rituals and Reminders

- **Savor Ritual:** Each night, light a candle or sip your tea slowly. Recall one moment from the day that made you smile, even faintly.
- **Gratitude Photo Challenge:** Take a photo of something ordinary you're grateful for each day. Save them in a folder—just for you.
- **Joy Anchor:** Wear or carry a small object that reminds you of a moment you liked in your life. Whenever you feel pulled into comparison, touch it as a reminder: "This is mine. I like it here."

## The Myth of "Settling"

Let's bust the myth that contentment is giving up. Contentment is not the end of growth—it's the beginning. When you root into what's already good, you grow from a place of wholeness, not lack.

You're less likely to make desperate choices or chase things that don't fit.

Contentment is not a vow to never change.
It's the courage to look at your life with honest eyes and say: "This is enough for now. I am enough for now. And wanting more doesn't mean I have to hate what is."

## You Don't Need a Breakthrough to Belong to Your Own Story

You don't need to be more evolved, more healed, more impressive.
You just need to notice your life again.

And when you do?
You'll remember: this lane, this breath, this weird, beautiful, unfinished little life?
It's enough.

Because you're enough.
And you always have been.

# ✦Chapter 14✦
# Comparison Across Cultures: Identity, Heritage, and the Myth of the "Right Way"

If you've ever felt like you're too much, not enough, or just plain "wrong" for the culture(s) you inhabit—welcome to the club. Comparison doesn't just happen at the individual level; it plays out across cultures, communities, and generations, shaping who we think we should be.

## The Cultural Comparison Game

Maybe you grew up straddling two worlds—your family's heritage and the culture outside your door. Maybe you're the first in your family to go to college, or you speak a language at home that your friends don't understand. Maybe your traditions don't fit the mainstream, or you're constantly fielding questions about "where you're really from."

Cultural comparison is sneaky. It tells you there's a "right way" to belong, succeed, love, or even grieve. It whispers,

"You're too different," or "You're not doing it right," or "You'll never fit in."

## The Myth of Assimilation

Assimilation is the ultimate comparison trap. It promises belonging—if you just shave off your edges, mute your accent, or trade your grandmother's recipes for avocado toast.

But here's the truth: You can't perform your way into true belonging. The more you compare, the more you lose touch with the parts of you that are actually magic.

## Heritage as a Source of Power (Not Shame)

Your story—your name, your rituals, your family's weird traditions—isn't something to hide or "fix." It's your birthright. The moment you stop comparing your culture to the "norm" is the moment you start coming home to yourself.

# Comparison and Identity: Intersectionality as Strength

Race, gender, sexuality, ability—these are not boxes to check or obstacles to overcome. They are sources of wisdom, perspective, and resilience. The comparison trap wants you to rank yourself in systems that were never designed for you to win.

But your identity isn't a liability. It's a lens that lets you see what others miss.

## Detox Practice: Celebrate Your Contradictions

1. **Name What Makes You Different.**
   Write a list of the ways your background, identity, or culture sets you apart. Then, flip the script—how are these your superpowers?
2. **Find Your People.**
   Seek out stories, communities, and mentors who reflect your lived experience. You don't have to be the only one.

3. **Honor Your Traditions.**
   Cook the food, speak the language, keep the rituals—whatever feels like home. Comparison can't survive in the light of true belonging.

4. **Challenge the "Right Way."**
   Every time you catch yourself thinking, "I should do this like them," ask whose rules you're following—and whether they serve you.

## Reflection Break

- Where do I feel most "outside" or "different"?
- How have I tried to fit in by comparison or assimilation?
- What would it look like to honor, rather than hide, my heritage and identity?

## The Power of Being Unapologetically You

You don't have to be the poster child for your culture—or anyone else's. You just have to be real. The world needs your stories, your flavors, your perspective. The right way? It's the way that feels like home in your bones.

# ✦Chapter 15✦
# The Power of Play, Rest, and Pleasure in a Comparison Culture

Let's get one thing straight: Burnout is not a badge of honor, and "busy" is not your personality. In a world addicted to achievement, play, rest, and pleasure are downright radical. They're also the ultimate antidotes to comparison.

## Play: The Lost Art of Joy for Joy's Sake

Remember when you were a kid and nobody cared if you were "good" at hopscotch or if your mud pies were Instagram-worthy? Play was about delight, curiosity, and being gloriously unproductive.

Comparison kills play. It turns everything into a performance. But the secret to unlocking creativity, courage, and connection? It's letting yourself have fun—without a scoreboard.

## Rest: The Ultimate Rebellion

Rest is a four-letter word in hustle culture. But you know what's sexy? Boundaries. Naps. Saying "no" to the grind and "yes" to your nervous system.

When you're rested, you remember who you are. You stop measuring, and you start living.

## Pleasure: The Permission Slip You Didn't Know You Needed

Pleasure isn't just about sex (although, let's be honest, that counts). It's about savoring—food, touch, movement, art, music, nature. It's about being in your body, not just performing it.

Comparison tells you pleasure is something you have to earn. But you don't. You're allowed to feel good, right now, for no reason at all.

## Detox Practice: Play, Rest, and Pleasure Challenge

1. **Schedule Play.**
   Do something silly, pointless, or completely unproductive this week. Dance in your kitchen.

Finger-paint. Build a pillow fort. Your inner child will thank you.

2. **Prioritize Rest.**

   Take a nap. Say no to an obligation. Go to bed early. Let yourself be "lazy"—and notice how your creativity comes back online.

3. **Indulge in Pleasure.**

   Make a list of simple pleasures. Tea. Sunshine. Good sheets. A long shower. Give yourself permission to enjoy them, unapologetically.

## Reflection Break

- When was the last time I played, just for fun?
- How does rest (or the lack of it) affect my self-comparison?
- What pleasures am I denying myself because I think I haven't "earned" them?

## Your Joy Is Not a Luxury

You don't have to hustle for your happiness. Play, rest, and pleasure are your birthrights. In a world obsessed with comparison, choosing joy is the most radical thing you can do.

# ✦Chapter 16✦

## When Comparison Gets Spiritual: Faith, Meaning, and the Search for "Higher Vibes"

Just when you think you've outgrown comparison, it slips in through the incense smoke and chanting playlists. Suddenly, meditation is a contest, your yoga practice is a performance, and even your "healing journey" starts to feel like a race to enlightenment. You set out hoping to find peace, only to discover you're now worried about being the most peaceful person in the room.

Let's be real: the spiritual path, in all its forms, is fertile ground for comparison. From faith communities to wellness retreats to the "manifestation" corners of social media, the search for meaning and connection can turn competitive—fast.

### Spiritual Bypassing and the Enlightenment Arms Race

Let's call it what it is: spiritual spaces aren't immune to comparison. In fact, sometimes they amplify it.

Who's the most "woke"?

Who's manifesting fastest?

Who eats the cleanest, vibrates the highest, or posts the most Buddha quotes?

Who's transcended all earthly desires (while still charging $999 for a course on abundance)?

The search for meaning becomes another tightrope to walk, another metric to measure, another way to feel behind.

**This is the "enlightenment arms race."**

You're not less evolved because you still get jealous, angry, or want to throat-punch someone at Whole Foods. You're just human.

# The Illusion of "Spiritual Achievement"

It's easy to confuse spiritual growth with spiritual achievement.

But there's no enlightenment trophy, no "Best in Class" for awakening, and no cosmic leaderboard keeping score.

When our search for meaning becomes competitive, we lose the heart of the journey: the honest, raw, messy work of being human and loving ourselves anyway.

## The "Good Vibes Only" Trap

Toxic positivity is the spiritual version of the highlight reel.
It tells you to "choose joy," "raise your vibration," "let it go"—all while shaming you for having actual feelings.

**Newsflash:** True healing isn't about bypassing your darkness. It's about loving yourself right in the middle of it.

- You're not failing if you still have bad days, get triggered, or need to process old wounds.

- You're not "low vibe" because you feel grief, anger, jealousy, or doubt.

- You're not unworthy of spiritual belonging because you're still a work in progress.

# The Science of Spiritual Bypassing

Psychologist John Welwood coined the term "spiritual bypassing" to describe using spiritual ideas and practices to avoid facing unresolved emotional issues.
Research shows that people who allow themselves to feel and process hard emotions—not just plaster over them with "good vibes"—are actually more resilient, compassionate, and content in the long run.

# Comparison in Faith Communities

Whether you're part of a church, a temple, a mosque, a meditation group, or just a group chat called "Witchy Book Club," faith can be fertile soil for comparison.
Who volunteers the most?
Who prays the most?
Who forgives most easily?
Who's the "best" believer?

But the divine doesn't keep score.
And you don't have to either.

# The Double-Edged Sword of Belonging

Faith communities offer belonging, support, and shared meaning—but they can also breed subtle competition.

- Who's most devoted?
- Who quotes scripture best?
- Who's "in" and who's "out"?

If you've ever felt "not spiritual enough," "not devout enough," or "not enlightened enough" in your own faith home, you're not alone.

Remember: **Spirituality is an inside job.**
Your path is sacred—not because it's visible or impressive, but because it's yours.

## Detox Practice: Spiritual Sovereignty

Ready to reclaim your spiritual journey from comparison?
Try these practices:

## 1. Unfollow the Gurus

If someone's teachings make you feel "less than," it's okay to take a break.

- Unsubscribe, unfollow, or mute voices that feed your insecurities instead of your soul.
- Remember: No teacher, influencer, or guru knows your path better than you do.

## 2. Honor Your Mess

Journal about the parts of you that don't feel "high vibe." Offer them compassion instead of judgment.

- What if your sadness, anger, or confusion is not a failure, but an invitation to wholeness?
- What if "shadow work" is just as sacred as "light work"?

## 3. Redefine "Progress"

Spiritual growth isn't linear.
Celebrate the setbacks, the stuckness, and the days you just want to eat carbs and binge reality TV.

- Progress might look like crying in your car, setting a boundary, or just getting out of bed.
- Spiritual maturity is not constant bliss—it's radical acceptance of your entire self.

# 4. Find Your Own Meaning

Whether it's prayer, meditation, walks in nature, or screaming into a pillow—your connection is sacred, no matter what it looks like.

- You don't have to chant, journal, or sage your space if it doesn't feel true to you.
- Define your rituals by what brings you home to yourself, not what looks good on Instagram.

## Reflection Break

- Where do I compare my spiritual or healing journey to others?

- What practices genuinely nourish me, and which ones feel performative?

- How can I make space for my humanity in my search for meaning?

Write freely. Be honest. Give yourself permission to be as messy and miraculous as you really are.

# Permission to Be a Work in Progress

You don't have to be a guru to be worthy.

You don't have to "ascend" to belong.

Your spiritual path is as messy, weird, and beautiful as you are—and that's enough.

## Embodying Spiritual Enoughness

- **Affirmation:** "I am allowed to be spiritual and imperfect. My messy humanity is not a flaw—it's my greatest teacher."

- **Daily Reminder:** Place a note somewhere you'll see it: "I am enough, even when I'm not enlightened."

- **Community Check:** Surround yourself with people who value honesty over performance, humility over hierarchy, compassion over competition.

# Final Word: Your Sacred, Unfinished Journey

Remember:

The divine doesn't keep score.

Your path doesn't have to look like anyone else's.

Your "higher vibe" is not a contest—it's a coming home.

You are allowed to be a beautiful work in progress.

Messy. Searching. Sometimes lost.

Always enough.

# ✦Chapter 17✦

# Digital Detox, Boundaries, and the Art of Sacred Unfollowing

Let's face it: Your phone is a comparison machine. Every ping, swipe, and scroll is an invitation to measure yourself against the entire world. Your screen glows with other people's vacations, highlight reels, launches, milestones, and "just woke up like this" selfies. Even your favorite memes can become a sneaky yardstick for how fun or clever you're supposed to be.

But here's the radical truth:
**You are allowed to curate your digital life the same way you do your real one.**

## The Power of Unfollowing

Somewhere along the way, we absorbed the idea that "unfollowing" is rude, dramatic, or petty. But let's reframe:

- You don't owe anyone your attention.

- Not the influencer who triggers your insecurity.

- Not the high school acquaintance who only posts family vacation slideshows.

- And definitely not the ex who "accidentally" watches all your stories but never reaches out.

**Unfollowing is self-care. Muting is emotional hygiene.**
You're not being petty—you're protecting your peace.

## Why Unfollowing Feels So Hard

Research shows that digital connection activates the same social circuitry in the brain as real-world relationships. That's why unfollowing can feel like a social risk—even when it's just an algorithmic adjustment. But your brain will thank you for less noise, less comparison, and more intentional connection.

## Boundaries: The Digital Kind

Boundaries aren't just for people. They're for platforms, apps, and algorithms that feed you a steady diet of not-enoughness. You're allowed to say no.

**Here's how:**

- **Set limits:** No screens after 9 p.m. No doomscrolling before coffee. Try a "one-screen-at-a-time" rule.

- **Delete the app:** Even just for a weekend. See what happens when the urge to check is replaced with the urge to rest or create.

- **Curate your feed:** Follow people who inspire, inform, or make you laugh—unapologetically. Fill your feed with artists, thinkers, and real friends, not just influencers and ads.

## The Science of Attention

Studies show our attention spans are shrinking—and our anxiety is rising—with every notification. Your attention is a precious, limited resource, and every time you let an app or algorithm steal it, you lose a bit of your focus, clarity, and peace.

**Restoring your attention is a spiritual act.**

# The Art of Restoring Your Attention

Your attention is sacred. It's the most valuable thing you own.

Every time you reclaim it, you remember who you are—outside the noise.

**Try this:**

- Notice how often you reach for your phone out of habit, not intention.

- Practice "single-tasking"—give your full focus to one thing at a time, whether it's a conversation, a meal, or just sitting with your thoughts.

- Replace idle scrolling with intentional pauses: stretch, breathe, step outside, or simply look around.

## Digital Minimalism

You don't have to go full "flip phone in the woods." Start with a few mindful choices:

- Move apps off your home screen.
- Turn off non-essential notifications.

- Use "Do Not Disturb" for chunks of your day.

## Detox Practice: A Digital Sabbath

A "digital sabbath" is a sacred pause from online life—a chance to reconnect with the world beyond the screen.

**How to try it:**

1. **Pick a day, an hour, or a morning.** Decide when you'll go offline.
2. **Go all in:** No scrolling, no posting, no checking who liked your post. Airplane mode is your friend.
3. **Notice how you feel:** Awkward? Bored? Free? All of the above? Let the discomfort be a teacher, not a punishment.
4. **Fill your time with something nourishing.**
   - Read a book.
   - Walk in your neighborhood.
   - Nap without guilt.
   - Call a friend, bake banana bread, journal, or just sit in silence.
   - Anything but compare.

# What Happens When You "Unplug"

You may notice the urge to grab your phone, the itch to check "just in case." This is detox in action.

With time, you may also notice:

- Your mind slowing down.
- More focus and creativity.
- Less anxiety, more peace.
- A sense of coming home to yourself.

## Reflection Break

- Which accounts make me feel inspired, and which make me feel "less than"?
- How often am I online just to fill space—or avoid my own feelings?
- What would my life look like with more boundaries and less comparison?

Write your answers honestly. No judgment, just curiosity. Let this reflection guide your next digital steps.

# You Are Allowed to Unfollow

The digital world is loud, but your inner world is louder—if you make space to hear it.
Unfollowing isn't mean. It's medicine.
Muting is maturity.
Boundaries are a blessing.

**Your lane, your rules.**

## Micro-Practices for Digital Freedom

- **The "Joy Feed" Experiment:** Only follow accounts that spark joy or teach you something new. Do a 24-hour test: How does your mood shift?
- **Notification Fast:** Turn off notifications for all non-essential apps for one week.
- **Real-World Ritual:** Replace the first 10 minutes of your morning and the last 10 of your night with offline rituals. Stretch, breathe, or write a gratitude note.
- **"Unfollow Guilt" Letter:** Write (even if you never send) a thank-you/goodbye note to anyone

you unfollow. Release guilt and reclaim your peace.

## Final Word: Digital Peace is Possible

You are allowed to design a digital life that feels as nourishing as your real one.
You are allowed to log off, mute, unfollow, and say no to anything that steals your joy, your time, or your sense of enoughness.

Remember:
**You are not missing out.**
**You are tuning in.**
**You are not falling behind.**
**You are moving forward—on your terms.**

# ✦Chapter 18✦

# Real-Life Stories: How Others Detoxed Comparison

Sometimes the best way to break the comparison spell is to hear from people who've been there, done that, and lived to tell the tale—messy, honest, and unfiltered.

## Story 1: Jess, 32—"I Unfollowed 200 People and Found My Voice"

"I realized I was spending more time watching other people's lives than living my own. The unfollow button felt scary, like I was burning bridges. But within a week, I noticed my anxiety drop. Suddenly I had space—mental, emotional, creative. I started painting again. I called my grandma. I remembered what my own voice sounded like. 10/10, would recommend."

## Story 2: Leo, 41—"I Stopped Competing With My Brother"

"My younger brother was always the 'golden child.' I spent years trying to outdo him—career, house, car, even hairline. It wasn't until my therapist asked, 'What if you're both enough?' that I let go. Now, I root for him. And for myself. We're finally real friends."

## Story 3: Priya, 28—"I Made My Own Traditions"

"As a first-generation immigrant, I always felt caught between cultures. I compared everything—food, holidays, even my accent. When I stopped trying to do things the 'right' way, I started creating rituals that felt like home. My friends love coming over for Diwali... and tacos."

## Story 4: Sam, 37—"I Gave Up the Achievement Olympics"

"I used to think my worth was tied to my job title. After my layoff, I was humiliated. But losing that identity set me free—I wrote a book, started therapy, and realized success is just being able to look in the mirror and like what you see."

## Story 5: Mia, 25—"I Made Play a Priority"

"My anxiety always spiked after scrolling. I started doing 'play dates' with myself—roller skating, baking disasters, painting for no reason. I stopped caring about being good and just had fun. The less I compared, the more I came alive."

## Your Story Matters

These are just a handful of the thousands of ways people have detoxed from comparison. What's your story? Write it down. Share it. Or just live it, loud and proud.

## Reflection Break

- What's one comparison habit I've broken—or want to break?
- Who inspires me to be more myself?
- What would my 'after' story sound like?

**You did not come here to live someone else's story.**
**You came here to write your own.**

# ✦Final Blessing✦

## For the One Who's Ready to Be Enough Without a Benchmark

May you remember who you were before the scroll stole your sparkle.

Before you measured your timeline against hers.
Before you apologized for your softness.
Before you confused someone else's highlight reel for your purpose.

May you forgive yourself for shrinking.
For hesitating.
For ghosting your own gifts.
For trying to fit inside a blueprint that was never written for your kind of magic.

You didn't fall behind, love.
You just fell asleep to your own brilliance for a little while.
But you're awake now.

And that awakening?

It's not loud.

It's not viral.

It's not performative.

It's *quietly sovereign.*

The moment you stop comparing is the moment you start *belonging*—to your own voice, your own body, your own weird and wonderful life.

So here's what I hope for you now:

That you create what you want to create, even if someone else already did it.

That you take up space, even if someone else is louder.

That you wear the thing. Post the thing. Say the thing.

That you stop trying to catch up, and start building a life that feels like *you.*

May your milestones be soul-timed.

May your joy be unedited.

And may your enoughness be *non-negotiable.*

You don't need to be better.
You don't need to be her.

You just need to be *here*.
And baby, that's more than enough.

Always has been.

— *Sage & Belle*

# ✦Bonus Section✦

## Journal Prompts for Breaking the Comparison Loop

*Because clarity is your antidote, and self-honesty is your superpower.*

Use these prompts anytime you feel the noise getting loud again. Let them anchor you back into your truth.

1. Where in my life do I still feel like I'm "behind"? Whose pace am I secretly following?
2. What do I believe someone else has that I'm not allowed to have yet?
3. What does "enough" actually look and feel like to *me*—not my industry, family, or feed?
4. If I stopped trying to be impressive, what would I start doing more of? Less of?
5. What do I already love about my life that I've been overlooking?
6. What's something I'm proud of that nobody sees but me?

7. What would my life feel like if I stopped checking how it compares and started checking how it *feels*?

Write freely. Write messily. Write like you're remembering yourself—not proving anything to anyone.

# The Mirror Ritual

## A Detox Practice to Unhook from External Validation and Reclaim Your Self-Perception

This is a simple but powerful ritual to help you return to your body, your lane, and your enoughness.

**You'll need:**

- A mirror (handheld or full-length)
- A quiet space where you won't be interrupted
- A pen and a small notepad
- A willingness to see yourself without judgement

**The Practice:**

1. Stand in front of the mirror. Not to critique. Just to *witness*.

2. Look at yourself. Not just your features—look into your eyes. Stay for a beat longer than usual.

3. Out loud or silently, say:

> "This is me. This is now. And I'm enough here."

4. Write down 3 things you *like* about what you see—physical or energetic.
   Then write 3 things you're *grateful* to your body for today.

5. Take a breath. Smile if it feels right. Cry if you need to. Let it land.

Repeat weekly—or daily—until this version of you starts to feel like home again.

## Mantras for Staying in Your Lane

*Because your brain needs reminders. Often. And said out loud.*

Keep these somewhere visible. On your mirror. Your phone. Your fridge. Your heart.

"Her success isn't my failure."

"I don't need to catch up—I need to come back to myself."

"My pace is not a problem."

"My joy doesn't need an audience to be real."

"I am not behind. I am unfolding."

"There's room for all of us to win—especially when I'm winning as *me*."

"I'm not here to be better than her. I'm here to be fully *me*."

"My lane was never supposed to look like hers."

"Enough isn't a destination—it's a decision."

Speak them when you feel comparison creeping in.
Repeat them like medicine.
Let them become your rhythm.

# ✦Bibliography✦

*Sources of Inspiration, Insight, and Inner Liberation*

1. **Brown, Brené.** *The Gifts of Imperfection.* Hazelden Publishing, 2010.
— For insights on shame, vulnerability, and living authentically.

2. **Neff, Kristin.** *Self-Compassion: The Proven Power of Being Kind to Yourself.* William Morrow, 2011.
— A foundational source for self-kindness over self-criticism in healing.

3. **Tolle, Eckhart.** *The Power of Now.* New World Library, 1999.
— Referenced for presence-based living and detaching from egoic identity.

4. **Chopra, Deepak.** *The Seven Spiritual Laws of Success.* Amber-Allen Publishing, 1994.
— For inspiration around divine timing, detachment, and self-trust.

5. **Dispenza, Joe.** *Breaking the Habit of Being Yourself.* Hay House, 2012.

— Used in referencing how repeated thoughts and feelings wire comparison into our nervous system.

6. **Young, Caroline Criado.** *Invisible Women: Exposing Data Bias in a World Designed for Men.* Chatto & Windus, 2019.

— For understanding cultural systems that feed the comparison gap, especially in visibility and validation.

7. **Dr. Gabor Maté.** *When the Body Says No.* Vintage Canada, 2003.

— Referenced in relation to nervous system responses to stress, pressure, and unworthiness.

8. **Bréne Brown.** *Atlas of the Heart.* Random House, 2021.

— For emotional mapping of comparison, envy, shame, and belonging.

9. **Glennon Doyle.** *Untamed.* Dial Press, 2020.

— Cited for inspiration around owning one's lane and breaking free from social expectation.

10. **Clarissa Pinkola Estés.** *Women Who Run with the Wolves.* Ballantine Books, 1992.

— Referenced metaphorically for archetypes and reclaiming the wild self beyond performative living.

11. **Tara Mohr.** *Playing Big: Practical Wisdom for Women Who Want to Speak Up, Create, and Lead.* Portfolio, 2014.
    — For unpacking inner critics and the voices that block creative expression.

12. **Nedra Glover Tawwab.** *Set Boundaries, Find Peace.* TarcherPerigee, 2021.
    — Referenced in conversations around reclaiming your lane and setting internal rules for self-comparison.

13. **James Clear.** *Atomic Habits.* Avery, 2018.
    — Referenced briefly in practices for interrupting comparison-driven behavior loops.

14. **Social Psychology Research** (Various Authors)
    — For foundational concepts in social comparison theory, particularly the work of Leon Festinger.

15. **Kristin Keane.** "The Body Isn't a Problem to Solve." *Psychology Today*, 2019.
    — Referenced for compassionate reframe of body-based comparison and shame.

# ✦About The Author✦

**Belle Titmus** is a lifelong book lover with a soft spot for stories that make you think, laugh, and heal all at once. After years of reading self-help books that felt more like homework than hope, Belle began writing what she calls *bite-sized brilliance*—books short enough to read in one sitting but rich enough to leave a mark.

Her *Detox Series* distills the noise of modern life—comparison, approval, perfection, productivity—into clear, practical, and heartfelt truths you can actually use. With a mix of humor, insight, and a dash of rebellion, Belle's work reminds readers that self-growth doesn't have to be complicated to be life-changing.

When not writing, Belle can be found near water with a notebook, chasing quiet moments, and believing wholeheartedly that simplicity, honesty, and a touch of sass can change the world.